W9-AHT-818

A Gathering of Spirit

Women Teaching in American Buddhism

Primary Point Press
Cumberland, Rhode Island

A Gathering of Spirit
Women Teaching in American Buddhism

Bhikshuni Ane Pema Chödron
Ruth Denison
Maurine Myo-On Stuart, Roshi
Gesshin Prabhasa Dharma, Roshi
Dr. Joanna Macy
Jacqueline Mandell
Toni Packer
Barbara Rhodes, Ji Do Poep Sa Nim
Jan Chozen Bays, Sensei

Photo credits:
pages 15, 23, 27, 32, 46, 51, 60, 71, 75, 93, 95, 107 by Sonia Alexander
pages 3, 6, 7, 44 by Ruth Klein
pages 103, 112 by Anthony Manousos
page 64 by Ellen Sidor
page 111 by Ernie LeVesque
page 40 courtesy of Toni Packer
page 85 courtesy of Joanna Macy
page 31 courtesy of Jacqueline Mandell

Primary Point Press logo designed by Grazyna Perl

Cover art by Grazyna Perl

Design by Ellen Sidor

Third edition produced by J.W. Harrington, Christia Madasci, Jayne Morris, Isabel Resende, and Reverend Carter West

The talk "Politics of the Heart," and the list of recomended books beginning on page 118, are reprinted here with permission of Jacqueline Mandell.

All the material in this book is taken from the Women in Buddhism conferences held in 1983, 1984 and 1985 at Providence Zen Center in Cumberland, Rhode Island. With the exception of the 1984 panel discussion and portions of the 1985 panel discussion, all the talks were presented in *Primary Point*, the international journal of the Kwan Um School of Zen.

Printed in the United States of America,
on recycled paper using soy-based ink

First edition, 1987
Second edition, 1989
Third edition, 1992

ISBN 0-942795-05-9

A Gathering of Spirit

Women Teaching in American Buddhism

Some people say the end of the world is coming. But when an old age is finished, a new age begins. Human beings are part of the natural cycle, and this is a changing time for all species. This is the beginning of the age when women will control everything, just as men have up till now: the house, the family, politics, the economy. Soon there will be many more women leading their countries. Women will become as strong as men, as it was many thousands of years ago. This change from yang to yin has already begun.

When Bodhidharma came to China, he became the first patriarch of Zen. As the result of a "marriage" between Vipassana-style Indian meditation and Chinese Taoism, Zen appeared. Now it has come to the West, and what is already here? Christianity, Judaism, and so forth. When Zen "gets married" to one of these traditions, a new style of Buddhism will appear.

Perhaps there will be a woman patriarch, and all Dharma transmission will go only from woman to woman. Why not? So everyone, you must create American-style Buddhism. Get enlightenment!

Zen Master Seung Sahn

Contents

Acknowledgements

Without the hard work and enthusiastic support of a number of people, this book would not have appeared. We wish to express profound appreciation to Zen Master Seung Sahn, without whose dedicated efforts the Kwan Um School of Zen and Providence Zen Center would not be in existence today, a teacher who continually challenges his students to keep questioning and practicing. We would like to thank the Providence Zen Center, its directors, staff and residents, for their work in planning, publicizing, and running the three "Women in Buddhism" conferences. And to all those who attended the conferences, thanks for their enthusiasm and sharing, for it was their heartfelt response to the teachers and each other that encouraged us to continue the conferences and work toward their publication. A special note of thanks to Suzanne Bowman, former director and longterm resident at Providence Zen Center, who was the driving force behind the conferences.

We wish to thank all of the women teachers for their participation and cooperation in the editing of their talks. Eight teachers are fully represented here, but a strong contributor to the 1984 conference was Ruth Denison, a senior Vipassana teacher who founded Desert Meditation Center in Joshua Tree, California. Due to unfortunate taping and editing problems, we are unable to present her talk, but her contributions to the 1984 panel are included.

We would like to thank the staff of *Primary Point*, the journal of the Kwan Um School of Zen, in which these talks originally appeared, and especially former art director Mel Ash for all his help with the production of the first edition of this book. A big thank-you goes to the transcribers of the talks. Last, but not least, our appreciation goes to the office staff of the Kwan Um School of Zen, who in the throes of an already overcrowded schedule found a small publishing company, Primary Point Press, springing up in their midst overnight, like a mushroom after a hard day's rain.

There is no organization that springs forth without roots. Like-

Acknowledgements

wise there is no book that does not have its ancestors. In noting where this book has come from, we would like to especially acknowledge the Naropa Institute for its pioneering work in holding the first symposium in North America on women and Buddhism in 1982. And we salute the founders and members of the Kahawai collective at the Diamond Sangha in Hawaii, who started publishing *Kahawai—Journal of Women and Zen* in 1979 as "a forum and network for women in Buddhist meditation practice." We refer our readers to *Kahawai* journal (especially volume 5, number 4, Fall 1983) for a more complete account of the 1983 conference at Providence Zen Center. ❏

Preface to the Third Edition

In this third edition of *A Gathering of Spirit*, we have updated the biographies of the contributors and reset and enlarged the type throughout the book to make it more readable. Six years have passed since it was first written. This is an opportunity to note what progress has been made on the issues raised in the three historic Women in Buddhism conferences at Providence Zen Center.

First of all, we wish to mark the passing of one of our contributors, Maurine (Freedgood) Stuart, Roshi, who died February 26, 1990. A wonderfully sane and vigorous intelligence has passed from this world. No one who listened to her forceful, humorous Dharma talks, or practiced with her over the years at the Cambridge Buddhist Association or elsewhere will soon forget this gifted teacher. We hope her students will continue her tradition of passionate and courageous practice.

Secondly, three of our contributors have published one or more new works (Joanna Macy, Toni Packer and Bhikshuni Pema Chödron), and all of them (except for Maurine Stuart, Roshi) are still actively teaching and leading retreats. The rising tide of interest in women and Buddhism has continued and has manifested as a virtual torrent of books and articles by and about women practicing and teaching, and on the difficult issue of abuse of authority. This is an exciting surge of information to have available. You will find a comprehensive list in Jaqueline Mandell's list of recommended readings, which we are delighted to say she has greatly expanded from her original group of fifty. The new list follows the conference reports.

Thirdly, three new women teachers (one in the United States and two in Poland) have recently been certified by the Kwan Um School of Zen, which for years has been dominated by male teachers. This trend is fortunately evident in other schools of Zen practice as well. These are encouraging signs both for the schools and for American Buddhism. We hope these favorable manifestations continue, because there is ample evidence that American culture, indeed the entire globe, is in the throes of an extremely violent time in history. We desperately need the unique point of view that comes from women, who are the primary nurturers and socializing influences in our culture. With war, environmental crisis, and hunger tearing apart human society, we need leaders, male and female, who understand how to transcend duality, how to avoid polarities, how to mediate disputes in ways that empower each side. We need to become leaders who are wise enough to be free from adversarial ways of viewing each other.

Of course, from the fundamental point of view, there is no difference between female and male. But in our particular embodiment, we are definitely women or men, inevitably conditioned by our gender identity and experience.

The unique contributions of women

The premise of this book is that Buddhist women, both as teachers and practitioners, have immensely valuable gifts to offer in Dharma practice, and that the structure of American Buddhism allows women to assume leadership roles. Here are women who have stepped forward to lead in their sanghas, who by their presence and ability will encourage others to do the same. Women who prefer to work in the background, in supporting roles, teach in their own ways. What is most important is that women have equal opportunity to choose among various roles. Studies of corporate leadership have shown that men are groomed and actively supported by networks and by older mentors on virtually every step of the path towards authority. If we want this suffering world to benefit more fully from the gifts of wisdom and experience that women have, we must learn how to support each other on the path to leadership. Women's spiritual authority needs to be manifested and acknowledged in the very highest religious roles and offices.

In order to begin solving the world's great problems, we need the widest possible view. For example, Joanna Macy shows us how, if we are to effect large changes, we must consider and respect the whole non-human world. If we open ourselves fully to the earth, the earth itself will teach us what is required in order to care for and protect it. The brilliance of Joanna's recent proposal to create a nuclear guardianship project is an example of the perspective Buddhist women teachers bring to the problems of this world. We might call this "deep nurturing."

Historically, Buddhism stands out from the other great world religions in having created a monastic community of nuns who practiced the Buddha's way, and received and transmitted his teaching. However, these first women demonstrated their sincerity in a heroic barefoot walk of many days, and still had to petition the Buddha several times for their inclusion. While there were many obstacles to their achieving their spiritual goal, as Susan Murcott states in her recent book, *The First Buddhist Women*, "In Buddhism women can form celibate communities, teach, be ordained and ordain, preach, gather disciples and create religious poetry of great force." Buddhism has always been fettered by the sexism of the patriarchal cultures in which it flourishes, but the teaching of the Buddha Dharma acknowledged from the start that women have the same capacity as men to realize religious truth.

The task of the new Buddhism

Among the problems that American Buddhists urgently need to address are issues of abuse of religious authority, about which there has been much current debate. What's healthiest in all of this is that the silence at last has been broken. Diana Rowan, in her excellent "Open Letter to the American Buddhist Community" in *Turning Wheel* (summer 1991), compares the "conspiracy of silence" (the net of secrecy and denial which Buddhist organizations have tended to pull around their dysfunctional behaviors) with the silence of the Chinese regime in regard to human rights abuses in Tibet.

And whenever abuse occurs in our religious institutions, we *all* have some responsibility for having tolerated or ignored the conditions that made it possible. In this book there are awakened voices of women who do not just address these issues reactively, but speak from a space of clear awareness and maturity. Abuse of power is not the Dharma, it is simply abuse of power.

It seems clear that some basic organizational changes need to be made, if structures and conditions in our schools and centers still allow abuses to happen. Can organizations or clans be formed that will work, that have the elements of the circle, power with others instead of always over others? Can we produce and select female and male teachers wise enough to know (or listen to those who see) when they are being seduced by the trappings of authority? And there are personal changes, too, that need to be made, changes in our own practice and the way we approach it. When we as American Buddhists are able to regard ourselves as so *ordinary* that we are willing to subject our business, social, and religious practices to basic ethical egalitarian standards, we will no longer participate in creating potentially abusive situations in our institutions.

Since Buddhism is a vehicle for true human liberation, we must take meticulous care in how it evolves and be relentlessly willing to discard what is not working. This means continually returning to the drawing board: the Buddha's original teachings, the authority of our individual experience. The koan of the present is the same one that human beings have had to face throughout history: can we learn how to function compassionately without being trapped by our rage, greed, and illusions?

In her wonderful book, *Everyday Zen*, Charlotte Joko Beck points to the tremendous courage involved in following the Dharma. That courage and the clarity arising from Buddhist practice, and the emphasis on realizing truth as it is, can propel us through our most difficult problems. But we must clearly see that these problems are not separate from the Dharma, they too are its content. As the ancient metaphor goes, the lotus blossom springs forth from its roots in the mud. In other words, we will always be in the midst of working things out.

During the Buddhist teacher scandals of the mid-80's, I asked Zen Master Seung Sahn what he thought about all this. After reflecting a moment, he said, "New shoots break the ground." Perhaps it helps to see that from its beginnings in this country over 100 years ago, American Buddhism has always been about old ground and new shoots. May we celebrate both as indissoluble parts of one another.

The women who have contributed to this book are themselves new shoots breaking the old ground, all proclaiming the message that there is a way to freedom. Here are freedom's rich and varied voices.

Ellen S. Sidor and Trudy Goodman

April, 1992

As Editor-in-Chief of Primary Point, *Ellen Sidor edited the original conference talks included in this book. Trudy Goodman, a psychotherapist and longtime Buddhist practitioner, led a workshop at the first Women in Buddhism conference, and shares Ellen's concern for women's issues in Buddhism.*

Recommended books and periodicals

Everyday Zen—Love and Work by Charlotte Joko Beck (Harper & Row, 1989)

The First Buddhist Women by Susan Murcott (Parallax Press, 1991)

Meetings with Remarkable Women—Buddhist Teachers in America by Lenore Friedman (Shambhala, 1987)

Not Mixing Up Buddhism—Essays on Women and Buddhist Practice by members of the Kahawai collective, Diamond Sangha, Hawaii (White Pine Press, Fredonia, NY, 1986)

Sakyadhita: Daughters of the Buddha by Karma Lekshe Tsomo (Snow Lion, 1988)
Sex in the Forbidden Zone by Peter Rutter (Jeremy Tarcher, 1989)
Turning the Wheel—American Women Creating the New Buddhism by Sandy Boucher (Harper & Row, 1988)
The Wisdom of No Escape by Pema Chödron (Shambhala, 1991)
Women in Buddhism, special issue (Vol. 6, #1,2,3) of *Spring Wind, Buddhist Cultural Forum* (Zen Lotus Society, Toronto, Ontario, Canada, 1986) .
World as Lover, World as Self by Joanna Macy (Parallax Press, 1991)
The Work of This Moment by Toni Packer (Shambhala, 1990)
Zen in America: Profiles of Five Teachers by Helen Tworkov (North Point Press, 1989)

Journals or newsletters which have published recent articles on the topic of abuse of power:

Dharma Gate—newspaper of One Mind Zen Center
Tricycle—The Buddhist Review
Turning the Wheel—The Buddhist Peace Fellowship Journal
Blind Donkey—Journal of the Diamond Sangha

Introduction

In looking at the growth of Buddhism in America, it seems the lake has come to the swans. Such a rich variety of teachers and traditions! In the last quarter of a century as American Buddhism has gone through a period of rapid gestation, women have begun to play more of a full and equal role in the process. As a result, there has been a tremendous qualitative change in the structure and forms of Buddhism in America.

In Asia for thousands of years, for cultural and historical reasons, there was a segregation between monks and nuns, between monastics and laypeople. There was a rigid sense of hierarchy; women were relegated to roles as devout supporters, rather than as equals or leaders. In America since the first arrival of Buddhism almost a century ago, women have practiced meditation together with monks and other men. Mrs. Ruth Fuller Sasaki (among others) set a shining example of a new type of American woman, demanding equality and practicing on her own terms. In the 1970's and 1980's, as Buddhist meditation found fertile soil and took stronger root in America, many women were drawn to it.

Inevitably, new shoots appeared. In some Buddhist communities, the number of women practitioners equalled and sometimes outnumbered male practitioners. Under the powerful influence of the Buddha's teaching of "no discrimination," women began to take and be given leadership roles, to define their own issues. Many felt dissatisfaction about their practice, a feeling which often arose from the difficulties of integrating formal practice and everyday life.

In the middle of the often frantic and frustrating juggle of community life, jobs, families, relationships, and the quiet and powerful allure of the meditation room, women meditators began to look for female role models. What was often felt as an individual "problem" was in fact the upwelling of an almost universal desire to find and get close to women teachers. But there were no established forums or networks in America for women in Buddhism, as there are in Judaism and Christianity. There was no list of approved teachers. The idea of holding a conference that would gather together and acknowledge women teachers and practitioners of Buddhism struck a lively chord.

In 1982 the Naropa Institute held an historic conference in Boulder, Colorado: the first American symposium on women and Buddhism. It drew many women and men and generated a lot of interest in continuing the networking, particularly among women, that the symposium had begun. Several conferences were tentatively planned for 1983 for different parts of the country, but the only one that materialized was the June 1983 conference at Providence Zen Center, entitled "The Feminine in Buddhism." It was the first of three such conferences inviting solely women teachers.

The person most directly responsible for the conferences at Providence Zen Center was Suzie Bowman, a longterm resident who from 1979 through 1982 was its director. A large part of her job was doing publicity, planning programs, and inviting guest speakers. As a result, by 1982 Suzie had been in contact for several years with a wide variety of women and men practicing and teaching Buddhism, and had spent considerable time networking on the telephone. That year she also became Head Dharma Teacher at Providence Zen Center and was responsible for running the formal practice at the Center. She described it as a very exciting time personally, because after years of focusing outward to other Buddhist communities and individuals, her job now was to focus inward on the residential and practicing community itself.

She was married to one of the teachers and struggling, as were many meditators across North America, to raise children in semi-monastic settings which were not especially knowledgeable or flexible about the demands of family life. Inevitably there were strains. Men and women in the teaching hierarchies tended to view personal problems as arising from not enough formal practice, so there was not much openness to questioning the systems themselves or their relationships to families.

Ellen Sidor

During that year Suzie joined a group of Buddhist women meditators which had recently formed in the Boston-Cambridge area. The women were or had been training with a variety of teachers, mostly male, although about half of them sat occasionally with Maurine (Freedgood) Stuart, Roshi, at Cambridge Buddhist Association. The group met monthly at different members' houses, meditated together, and discussed their experiences and feelings about living and practicing in their various situations. It soon became clear that many Buddhist communities were going through a similar process, which Suzie termed "a sort of adolescence"—a restlessness and questioning of the rigidity and authority of the mostly, but not in all cases, male-dominated hierarchies. Through this group and similar ones that had been formed, some as a direct result of the Naropa symposium, women meditators began to find a common voice.

In that same year Suzie met Susan Murcott, a woman whose religious search had led her from a Boston feminist Christian group to Japan, Australia, Hawaii, and back to Boston. Susan had been instrumental in founding the Kahawai collective at Diamond Sangha (under Robert Aitken Roshi) which began publishing Kahawai, Journal of Woman and Zen in 1979. Suzie invited Susan to the Providence Zen Center as a guest speaker. Susan gave a short introductory talk and then broke up the audience into small discussion groups, so that people could share in a more intimate setting their feelings about practicing in the community. The next day there was a luncheon for her, for women only. At the time, it felt quite revolutionary.

Following her visit and that of Toni Packer, who had just resigned her position of responsibility at Rochester Zen Center and started her own Zen Center, a women's group formed at Providence Zen Center. The women now had a forum, a place where they could share their experiences and importantly, their feelings. From this new consensus and closeness came a quiet strength and liveliness that flowed back out into the community. The idea of holding a Buddhist women teachers' conference at Providence Zen Center quickly gained support.

As planning at the Zen Center for the conference proceeded, we found that there were quite a few more women Buddhist teachers than we had known about. Suggestions were made, lists drawn up, invitations sent out. The 1983 conference was a one-day event. Some seventy women and some men attended. It was a warm and exuberant conference and people expressed strong desire for another one.

The 1984 conference spanned two days and wove periods of practice (meditation, chanting, and movement) together with talks, workshops, small group meetings, and a panel discussion. Over 120 people attended. There was a lot of good energy and many people from the previous year's conference returned. A special feeling developed from the closeness of sharing important things, especially in small affinity groups that met three times during the weekend. The large gatherings were marked by intense concentration and feelings of fellowship. Great gusts of laughter rocked the meditation hall, as participants experienced the freshness of spiritual teaching presented by intelligent, charismatic, and often humorous women teachers.

But many people, including some of the teachers, felt that the conference had been too busy: too much talk, too tight a schedule, not enough unstructured networking time, and not nearly enough of what is really essential in Buddhist practice—silence. To provide that silence and more inner space, the 1985 conference was planned for a weekend with a three-day retreat preceding it, led by Maurine Stuart Roshi of Cambridge Buddhist Association. About forty-five people sat the retreat.

The night before the conference began, the coordinators met with the teachers to finalize the schedule. All three of the conferences had been initially planned in the same way: the Providence Zen Center directors decided on an overall theme, the teachers were invited to present their own topics, a rough schedule was planned in advance and confirmed at the teachers' meeting.

As we met together that night, a consensus soon appeared that the proposed schedule (which had been devised to allocate in a fair manner two days among five teachers, one teacher dropping out at the last minute) was too confining. There were too many little time slots. A feminist, organic model for the weekend was proposed, in which there would be room for spontaneous action and for developing meetings whose agenda could grow out of the expressed needs of the participants. Instead of a "conference" dominated by the planners (hierarchic structure) there would be a "gathering" that would evolve from the interplay between the teachers and the participants (organic structure).

Everyone agreed to throw out the original schedule. Each teacher got a half day that she could structure any way she wanted to. The entire gathering would meet Saturday night for a panel discussion, but the tiny time slots, the titled workshops, the rushed movement of participants were all gone. Unfortunately, we also lost the small sharing groups that had been the backbone of the previous conferences. Between the loss of those small group meetings and the general perceived lack of structure, tempers began to rise.

By Saturday night, a number of participants were angry. People who had come for a "conference" had gotten a "gathering" they didn't really know how to use. The coordinators weren't experienced enough in the feminist model to offer guidelines on how to use it. People who were experienced in "gathering" didn't get what they wanted initially, either. During the rest of the weekend, the gathering worked hard on these issues. It was quite a learning experience, and showed that we all have a lot of listening to do, not just among women and men, but among women of different backgrounds and expectations.

You will find in this book the authentic voice of a new spiritual culture: women practicing and teaching Buddhism in America. Never before in the history of Buddhism, and probably not since the long-ago days of the height of Goddess worship, have women played so prominent a role in directing their own spiritual lives. There are no dry, detached, or abstruse theorists here, but women whose words are vibrantly alive and grounded in daily practice, whose teachings touch us at the heart of our daily life: our love relationships, our families, our work, our spiritual strivings.

Things are changing so quickly in the world just now that in a short time some of the talks in this book may sound dated. If that happens, we hope you will still be able to read this book with an open mind and an appreciation of how fresh these words sounded in the turbulent mid-1980's. We believe that much of the material in this book is timeless: lively contemporary teaching resting on solid ancient roots. We hope that it will prove valuable to you in navigating the uncharted years ahead.

Ellen S. Sidor

Providence, Rhode Island
March 9, 1987

The 1983 Conference:

The Feminine in Buddhism

The Feminine in Buddhism

A report of the 1983 Conference

On a beautiful warm spring day in June 1983, some seventy women and men gathered at the Providence Zen Center to attend a one-day conference on "The Feminine in Buddhism." Five first generation American women Buddhists, representing the Vipassana tradition and several Japanese and Korean Zen traditions, led a relaxed and friendly day of talks, workshops, and an informal lunch by the pond. This conference and the Naropa Institute "Women in Buddhism" symposium of 1982 were among the first public forums to focus on women's roles in contemporary American Buddhism.

The speakers were the late Maurine Stuart, Roshi of the Cambridge Buddhist Association, recognized in 1982 as a successor to Soen Roshi; Susan Murcott, long-time member of the Diamond Sangha in Hawaii and a co-founder of *Kahawai, Journal of Women and Zen*; Barbara Rhodes, a Ji Do Poep Sa Nim (dharma master) in the Kwan Um School of Zen and teacher at Providence Zen Center; Jacqueline Mandell, a long-time Zen and Theravadan student teaching at Insight Meditation Society in Barre, Massachusetts; and Trudy Goodman, a Zen student and child and family therapist in the Boston area.

Edited versions or selections from all of the talks and the introduction to Trudy Goodman's workshop were published in the Fall 1983 (Vol. V, No. 4) of *Kahawai, Journal of Women and Zen.* (For information about ordering copies, please write to the Diamond Sangha, 2119 Kaloa Way, Honolulu, HI 96822.) The following account of the conference was published in the January 1984 issue (Vol. 1, No. 1) of *Primary Point.*

Jacqueline Mandell, a Vipassana teacher from the Insight Meditation Society, opened the program with a guided meditation.

Maurine Stuart, Roshi of the Cambridge Buddhist Association gave a powerful opening talk. Some quotes follow.

Report of the 1983 Conference

"Within our own time ... and in our own American culture, we are making a work of art ... we must know our backgrounds—Korean, Japanese, or Theravadan—and have been trained in them thoroughly, and then we will be free to make our own American expression, either as men or women ....

"We are not here to imitate each other. One of the frightening things I see sometimes is people who are destroying differences. What a pity. To reduce everything to a sameness in the cause of equality is foolish. We are here to speak about the feminine in Buddhism, which in no way excludes the masculine."

Roshi, who was a concert pianist for many years, strode back and forth in front of the audience as she answered questions. The audience, which included a number of men, responded with lively attention and laughter.

When someone asked, "Roshi, does your spouse meditate?" she replied, "No, he does not. Once upon a time when I was away at sesshin and somebody said, 'Does your family engage in this?' and

I said somewhat shamefacedly, 'I'm sorry; they do not.' And Soen Roshi *(her teacher)* jumped up and said, 'One in the family is enough!'"

Barbara Rhodes, JDPSN gave a talk on "Nurturing Ourselves and Our Families." With some delightful stories about her own life, she talked of the many important teachings she has had which helped her accept both the masculine and the feminine in herself. "Nurturing ourselves and our families is hard. We can't nurture ourselves unless we know who we are, and we can't know ourselves unless we let ourselves be. That can come about through sitting practice, but it also means opening up to the teachers that are here right now, whether they are Zen Masters or not." In conclusion she said, "Find that state of mind where we are no longer comparing, no longer feeling like a self, but being with what we are experiencing."

Power and integrity were key points in the talk given by Jacqueline Mandell. She said she finds herself in the position of wanting to help empower women. "What the Dharma has to offer to ourselves and to power is integrity, *i.e.* freedom from greed, ignorance and delusion ... In the moment of awareness, we are free of these." She told a story about a woman teacher from India who travels by herself a great deal, in a country and culture where this is not very acceptable for women. Asked how she dealt with people who would limit her, this teacher replied, "I just de-authorize them!"

The afternoon featured workshops run by five speakers. In Maurine Stuart, Roshi's group the participants were asked to speak to the question, "How do you act with compassion and wisdom in your everyday, practical life?" During the hour of discussion, Roshi answered many personal questions about whether to live at a Zen Center or not, having patience with oneself —and her answers always struck the heart of the question, and the questioner.

Trudy Goodman, child psychotherapist and Zen student, led the workshop on "Work and Family Life." The whole question of family life, she said, is the work of lineage and transmission. "Finding our lineage and deciding what it is that we want to transmit is an important step." She continued:

> *"Our lineage is not something that only happens in beautiful calligraphies in the Dharma room, starting with the Buddha and ending with the Zen Master. It's in our family albums, our family photographs, and in our lives right now .... A friend of mine, Sonya Margulies, once gave a talk at Berkeley Zendo which she began with a very moving ritual: she chanted the names of many important women in her life, adding after each name the Japanese honorific 'Dai Osho' .... Practice and work are not something that we impose on ourselves so that we have to be someone other than who we are. Looking into our lives, we can see work to do which expresses who we are."*

Susan Murcott's "Sexuality and Buddhism" workshop provided a format for participants to discuss the difficulties they encountered with sexuality in Buddhist communities. "In some Zen communities," she said, "there has been an inability to speak openly about sexuality." One participant summed up the workshop, saying "Zen practice needs to integrate, not repress, our very real needs for intimacy in various ways, and open discussion should be encouraged in community life."

Barbara Rhodes, JDPSN gave some of the background of the Providence Zen Center community in the workshop on "Community Living." She explained that Zen Master Seung Sahn came from a monastic system where monks or nuns lived together and had a regular daily practice. For the first time in his life, he encouraged lay people to live together under one roof. "In a very simple way, community living— in supporting a spiritual practice—helps you let go of your personal opinions and desires and help you to be exposed to many different ideas. It's fuel to learn about yourself." Group members aired their concerns about problems and families living with single people, and how to create the time and energy to nurture a marriage.

Jacqueline Mandell led the workshop on "Empowerment and Personal Acceptance." Group members were asked to mention qualities which they had been working on that empowered them and difficulties which were still ongoing.

Susan Murcott delivered the closing talk on "The Feminine in Buddhism." She was concerned with the "male-oriented myth and teaching in our Zen form," because as she said,

"We live to some extent according to the myths we choose ... Much can be gained from immersing oneself in the practice of an inherited tradition. But we have the power, even the responsibility, especially as the first

Left to right: Barbara Rhodes, Jacqueline Mandell, Susan Murcott and Maurine Stuart.

Buddhist generation in the West, to shape our own forms, to translate and interpret from that inheritance in the context of our own culture, creating a practice that truly fits.

"I've sat zazen for years in the tropics with a gentle old man. I've sat zazen with the heavy Rinzai style of no sleep and bitter cold. It's all Zen. It doesn't matter. We can shape our style."

The day ended with a brief practice representing each of the Buddhist traditions at the conference. Jacqueline Mandell led a loving kindness meditation. The four Great Vows were chanted by Maurine Stuart, Roshi in Japanese, and in English by Barbara Rhodes, JDPSN, as all the participants held hands in a large circle.

After the conference many people lingered on the grounds and stayed for dinner. The relaxed feeling from earlier in the day remained. Many people asked that the conference be repeated, perhaps for an entire weekend next time.

Quoting from Margot Wallach, a long-time Diamond Sangha member living in Cambridge, Massachusetts, who helped produce the conference issue of *Kahawai:*

> *"The last event of the day was a large sharing circle of all the conference participants. I was impressed with the number of women who said that the conference was the first opportunity they had had to discuss feminism and Buddhism together in a Buddhist center. There was a lot of excitement about the recognition of women's issues—especially what it is like to practice as a woman—as a legitimate topic for discussion among teachers and students and among community members. Many people said they were inspired by the conference to return to their various centers and communities and continue the dialogue through women's groups and sharing meetings. I felt that seeds were planted that will bear the fruit of women being more empowered in their practice, communities, and work."* ❏

The 1984 Conference:

Women and Buddhism in America

Compassion and Wisdom: Gentle and Strong

Maurine Myo-On Stuart, Roshi

Dear friends, who have come from all across the continent, it is really a wonderful experience to be here. Let us start this afternoon by chanting together. The chant is NAMU DAI BO SA. All of you who practice will know that when you chant you are not thinking, "What does this mean?"—no need for that. Chanting is zazen with voice, with your whole being, every pore of you breathing the sound.

Before we do it let me briefly tell you what it means. "Namu" means "to unite with." Namu: let us unite in one spirit, one mind, together. Unite with "dai," which ordinarily means "big," but here dai means the absolute, the ultimate ground of our being that is every single one of us. So to unite with this absolute in a Bodhisattva spirit (Bosa means Bodhisattva), for the sake of all sentient beings we are here. For the sake of all sentient beings we are chanting.

Myoku asked Rinzai: "Avalokitesvara has one thousand hands and each hand has an eye. Which is the real eye?"

Rinzai answered: "Avalokitesvara has one thousand hands and each hand has an eye. Which is the real eye? Now tell me quick!" Rinzai said in his wonderful style, "Quick! Tell me!"

Myoku pulled Rinzai from his seat, then sat in his place. Rinzai stood up and asked "Why?" Then he shouted, "Kaaaaaatz!" and pulled Myoku from his seat in turn and Myoku left the room quietly.

This Bodhisattva of compassion and wisdom has one thousand eyes to see the thousands of needs, and thousands of hands to help. As symbols of this, some Bodhisattvas also have eleven faces, so that they may see in all directions simultaneously. A direct response is made in this vivid Zen school of Rinzai, which is my school. Rinzai's response to this question of "Which is the real eye?" was immediate and spontaneous. Why? Why are you asking which is the true eye? Why are we here?

At a dinner party some weeks ago, my husband and I in the course of the conversation were asked, "What is your favorite question?" Mine is "Why?" Why am I using this story? Avalokitesvara with the thousand eyes and hands is all the different roles that each one of us here represents: man, woman, artist, friend, mother, lover, child, whoever. Every single one without exception is this true eye.

It is the moment to moment experience of being here together that is so vital to all of us. This is the life-giving and wisdom-making process: our being here together, looking at how we are engaged with one another, heart to heart, hara to hara, mind to mind, and each one of us answering this "why?" with the deepest expression of our own nature, our own experience, without any speculation about it.

There was a Rinzai school nun named Chido who was given inka, meaning she was allowed to teach. Some monks were a little hesitant about it. Is it alright for this lady to be up here, giving us a discourse on the Rinzai Roku? Is it alright for this piano player from Saskatchewan, Canada, to be up here giving you a talk on the Rinzai Roku? Is that okay?

So this nun Chido, the founder of Toku-ji, confronted the head monk, who did not at all approve of her being given inka. He decided to question her. "Ha! I'm going to trap her and see how stupid this lady is. She is not ready to be a Rinzai Roku teacher. Let's see." So he said to her, "In our line, one who receives the inka gives a discourse on the Rinzai classic. Can this nun teacher really brandish the staff of the Dharma in the Dharma seat?"

She faced him, and drew out her 10-inch knife, carried by all women of her warrior class. She held it up and said, "Certainly a Zen teacher of the line of the patriarchs should go up on the high seat and speak on this book, but I am a woman of the warrior line an⸍ I should declare our teaching when really face to face with t' drawn sword. What book should I need?" The head monk s⸍

"Before father and mother were born, with what then will you declare our teaching?"

The nun closed her eyes and sat perfectly still.

The presence of each one of you is teaching the Rinzai Roku. Your living dynamic, wonderful presence is your living Rinzai Roku and mine, standing here heart to heart. This is what Rinzai asked us to come to in his Rinzai Roku: no hanging onto words and phrases but coming to the living dynamic spirit. This is what we are here for. Looking into all your wonderful faces, I sense how far you have come to share this experience together, not just in a distance of miles but in life distance. What experiences have brought us here together?

As Suzanne told you, I come from the Cambridge Buddhist Association. I am the teacher there. I am most grateful to be there.

"Zen must be able to change its form from what it was centuries ago. What will happen to it in America?

The founders of the Cambridge Buddhist Association some 27 years ago were people like Daisetz Suzuki and Shinichi Hisamatsu and Elsie Mitchell and John Mitchell and some other wonderful friends. Dr. Hisamatsu and Dr. Suzuki have passed on, but they left us a wonderful heritage. One of the things that Dr. Hisamatsu said when the Cambridge Buddhist Association was founded was that it should be a non-sectarian place. So our house is not just a zendo, but a place for all people to come for the study and practice of Buddhism. The fact that I am a Zen teacher does not mean that it is just a Zen Center. It is for everyone.

Dr. Hisamatsu was a great Zen teacher himself. When I saw Soen Roshi on his last visit, he said, "Dr. Hisamatsu was a true roshi, a true old teacher. I learned so much from him." Dr. Hisamatsu stressed the flexibility of Zen. One must know something of its history to understand it, but one must be aware of its flexibility, the way it adapts itself to various circumstances. It is not rigid. Zen must be able to change its form from what it was centuries ago. How will Zen differ now from the past? What will happen to it in America?

What is happening to Zen in America is very interesting, from the standpoint of its history and looking at the present scene. Some things are sad, and because they are really difficult, they are making us grow up in our Zen practice. They are making us become less dependent, making us see things much more clearly.

So where does this begin, this independent spirit in Zen? Before it came to America, there was a great deal of feeling already in Japan that it should be less encrusted by temple emphasis, although there's nothing wrong with the temple. I'm happy you're building one here. But Zen should extend itself to lay people, not just men but women too. It should be extended to everyone.

One of the roshis who believed this implicitly was a man called Kosen. His birthdate was as early as 1816. He was extremely interested in Western culture and insisted that his monks go to the university and learn about other parts of the world, learn other languages, study other philosophies, in fact, open their minds. He was the teacher of Soyen Shaku, the first Zen teacher to come to America.

In 1893 Soyen Shaku came well prepared to a conference of religions in Chicago. He understood our language and a great deal of Western thought. In 1905 he returned to San Francisco, which of course is the place of the beginning of Zen practice in America. He was welcomed into the home of Mrs. Alexander Russell, who was the first person in America to study Zen. This wonderful woman did deep koan study with Soyen Shaku. Wonderful beginnings!

Another great lady in our American tradition is Elsie Mitchell. It was she who with Dr. Suzuki and Dr. Hisamatsu began the Cambridge Buddhist Association. To this day she is inconspicuously working with all of us there to help wherever there is a need

—a true Bodhisattva of compassion and wisdom. Soen Roshi said to me when I left New York, "Do not be so sad to leave. Find Elsie Mitchell in Massachusetts and you'll be alright." Indeed he was right.

In June of this year, a group of women in California gathered with me to experience a sesshin together as women. This was not my idea. It was their very good idea, something that they wanted to try. I said, "I am absolutely at your disposal. I am very fond of men and I love to have them with us but if you feel that there will be some special quality—something that we can do together as women—then let us do it and find out what happens." So we did.

I arrived one afternoon and there was a sparkling young woman from the Empty Gate Zen Center to greet me at the airport. We went almost immediately to a meeting of a group of women who had

---

"Some things are sad, and because they are difficult, they are making us grow up in our Zen practice."

---

worked very hard on this, among them Lenore Friedman, who is here with us at this conference. The next day we went off to a Vedanta retreat house in Marin County. This was already a beautiful beginning for our time together. The Vedanta retreat house was quiet, beautifully cared for, with wonderful white deer wandering around on the lawn, humming birds in every little flower — incredible paradise!

But the meditation room of this Vedanta center was not for us as Zen students. It was very heavily carpeted and each little tuft of carpet was full of rose incense. The windows would not open wide enough. We looked around and asked, "What shall we do?" We moved all the furniture out of the living room, which was right next door to the kitchen, right next door to the dining room. "How shall we deal with this?" we asked, all the noise of food preparation,

setting the tables and so on. "Will it work?"

It worked. Everything flowed into everything else in a wonderful way. We went from the zendo into the dining room, into the kitchen, and back to the zendo, and it was all clearly flowing.

Once last year in our zendo in Cambridge, I tried this. As teacher, I was the cook, the giver of the talks, the interviewer, etc. All day I just went from one room to another, from this place to that place; it too was a clear and flowing experience, as in California. The atmosphere became stronger and warmer, participants feeling less and less judgmental and more accepting of everything.

In the California retreat, somehow many of these women had been intimidated by sesshin atmosphere, and also were somewhat fearful because of certain things that have happened in relation to teachers. So we were feeling closer and freer.

We listened to Rinzai. We listened to Nansen and Joshu as if they were there, as they were. The spirit is here, not in ancient China, but present in our time and place, right here. We listened to Nansen telling Joshu that this calm and ordinary mind, this non-discriminating mind, is the way. We heard Rinzai encourage us to seek Buddha within ourselves, not as something we seek outside or are given by someone. We heard Rinzai telling us to free ourselves from him, free ourselves from attachment to him or any teacher. No attachment.

It is so easy for us to become attached to what we revere. We put someone up on a pedestal. Soen Roshi was absolutely adamant about that. He always said, "Do not put me in that place, I am just an ordinary monk. I have to practice harder than you. Please don't put me in that place. No attachment to me. Look at the universe, the stars, look at the moon, look at all this. Don't look to me." No matter how lofty the teacher, in so far as that presence is outside of us, it's not real. It's not our own treasure.

We came here as we came together in California sesshin to realize Rinzai in us. His wonderful shout is our shout of joy and celebration of life together. We heard his "why?" Endless dimension universal life wondering. This was Soen Roshi's phrase: endless-dimension-universal-life. No beginning, no end, just wondering with heart empty and open.

When one of my children started mathematics in her grade school, she had a remarkable teacher. On the report card this teacher wrote: "At the beginning of the term, Barbara caught the spirit of mathematics and wondered on." So, here we are capturing this joyful celebration of life together, and wondering on.

To go back to this matter of teachers for a moment, Dogen Zenji said, "If you cannot find a true teacher it is better not to practice." Who or what is the true teacher? Our practice, whatever it is, is our teacher. Not necessarily Zen practice. Everyone here has their own practice. Your life is your practice. Your life is your koan. Each one of us learns from that, if we listen deeply, if we're involved down to the bottom. This is our true teacher, the most venerable teacher: our practice.

And what is our attitude to this teacher? Are we sitting with thoughts of dependency, of gaining something, of grabbiness? Or are we sitting instead with this kind of mind that other women teachers have spoken about today, this open-hearted, not-knowing, giving-up-yourself practice? No grabbiness, no gaining idea, just moment after moment open.

When we had finished the California sesshin, we sat around outside in a circle and had a very intimate time together, really open-hearted, ready to share experience and feelings of freedom and deep compassion with one another. What came out of it were feelings of real strength with that compassion. There was our compassion and wisdom, gentle and strong: real women warriors cutting off all their delusions about what they could or could not be. There we were!!

Maurine Myo-On Stuart, Roshi, one of the foremost of contemporary American Zen teachers, died of cancer on February 26, 1990 in Cambridge, Massachusetts. She was 67. Her last words to her sangha were, "Please continue your practice. You know what to do." ❏

Women And Buddhism in America

Gesshin Prabhasa Dharma, Roshi

I am very happy to be here at this women's conference. I am also very happy to see some men here. I am always at a loss for titles for my talks. Because I don't prepare talks, I never know what is going to come through. So it was easiest to take the theme of the conference, then maybe I could say anything!

The truth is I don't know anything about women and Buddhism in America. The only woman I know is this one. So when I talk, I can only talk about myself, and I truthfully think this self is any one of us. Whatever we do and look at is really self looking at self.

Whenever we look at a thing from a certain vantage point, it is to the exclusion of all other aspects of that thing. That means, it is not the total aspect of a thing. When we simply talk as women in the relative world, it would not be the Buddhist practice or way. After all, what Shakymuni revealed to us is the way out of discrimination and conflict. Therefore he was a liberator and not a person who gave us more problems.

In fact, when we look at the universe or what we call the Dharma or ultimate reality, there are no problems. All problems are man- or woman- or human-made, and therefore they can only be resolved by us. We have individual karma, we also have collective karma, and we must look at it. If we think we have a problem, we must look at it from various positions or dimensions. One of the communication problems of the world is people talking from different dimensions or levels and assuming they are all speaking on the same level.

I went to a conference once at Roanoke College in Virginia as one of three speakers. The conference theme was "Beyond Apathy." (The organizers first called it "Apathy" and then thought that was too dismal.) There was a sequestered meeting for three days and on the last day it was open to the general student body. In the closed meeting were 20 panelists sitting in a circle. For two days I merely listened to the papers that the various panelists brought, about their understanding of apathy in universities. The panel was made up of local clergy, politicians, and business people as well as faculty from the university. The leader was the dean of the chapel.

After two days they noticed I hadn't said a word the whole time, so they asked me if I had anything to say. I said, my preparations for this conference were quite different from yours. I noticed you all brought well-prepared papers. I do just the opposite. I sit in the morning in my room and try to forget everything that's on my mind. So I came here with an empty mind. I have no opinions or views. I really don't even know what apathy is. But I was able to hear you all talking and what I hear is this: you're talking this way and that you don't really meet.

The complaints were that the businessman's children had left home. This was during the hippie time and they were not interested in his business. They despised his big home and Cadillac and felt threatened. The politician, who was a woman, also had complaints because the students were not interested in her particular form of politics. And so it went, with the churches and so forth.

Of course most of the panelists lived in town and slept in their homes. Several other speakers had requested hotel rooms. I was offered a little apartment in a dormitory and spent my time with the students, having my meals with them. I found them a most lively and interested bunch. Of course, they took great notice of me in (monk's) outfit. We had wonderful conversations together and I did not have the impression that they were apathetic.

I told the panel this and said what I had noticed was that the students did not share the panelist's particular programs. They have their own ideas and programs. Maybe you should look at their ideas and see if there is anything you can share, and not feel threatened by the fact that they don't buy your religious and political pro-grams. In fact, I said, your children that have run away from home are living in our Zen centers! So I could tell them a little bit of what some of their kids were really into.

I think the problems we create in the world are when we get stuck, on anything—a thing or an idea. The Buddha was in the same situation we are, faced with a religious and social structure that didn't sound right, didn't feel right to him. Also he had no role models. Therefore he went and sat alone under a tree. He even left the religious community he had joined and went out by himself.

So did Jesus. Even though we usually see Jesus nailed to the cross, I tell Christians, "You forget that he spent 40 days in the desert. What did he do there? He meditated, he was alone."

Every Zen master has emphatically told us or is telling us that only your own inner reality must be looked at. Do not seek anything extra. Every knowledge, every science, every wisdom we have in

---

"What Shakyamuni Buddha revealed to us is the way out of discrimination and conflict. Therefore he was a liberator and not someone who gave us more problems."

---

this world in fact comes out of meditation. If you look at anything at all in this world and trace it to its source, you must end up doing zazen.

That's the path I've taken. In my case it evolved naturally. I spontaneously meditated as a child. About seventeen or eighteen years ago I learned about the form of zazen. I did not come to zazen because I was searching, but as a result of experiences I had. I found the way of the Buddha to be identical with my experiences and I could relate to it, but not so much in the way it has been developed by various traditions and cultures.

I always have a tendency to go back to the root. You can do this in stages. Perhaps first you examine the root of your own lineage or tradition. Somehow I have always felt closer to the Chinese masters than the ones in my own lineage, which was Japanese. I see the beginning of Zen as having occurred in China. I can relate to that because we have the same situation here.

The way is the inner path. When we look at something, we must view it from at least two positions. One that we naturally do is the one of the relative world, what we call the common ordinary world of phenomena or manifestation. Most people only take this position, ignorant of the fact of the underlying essence (the truth). I don't have to tell you this because most of you as practicing Buddhists know very well what we call ultimate reality, or the absolute or the unborn or the Buddha nature. We all know in the absolute there is no discernment whatsoever. Nothing is distinguished. There is equality.

So how can the Buddha, who profoundly realized this and gave us a living example, be said to have made rules that discriminate between this and that? The discrimination and the scriptures which give us problems were made by others, later. The beginnings of women's liberation were probably during Buddha's time. You know that in the pre-Buddhist era women had no place in society. They were wives meant to bear sons to their husbands. If they didn't, their husband was free to take another wife that might bear him sons, because the prevailing view was that only a son could close the dead man's eyes. In the Hindu tradition, the law of Manu stated that a woman was first subject to the father, next to the husband, and when the husband died, to her son.

It was at that time and place in history that the Buddha appeared and liberated women from this bondage. In the Dharma there is no discrimination of sexes or of anything. However, in the world of form, where this essence manifests as form, there are differences. There are men and women and millions of other manifested forms. What we have to see is that which is equal and free of discrimination, is simultaneously in its manifested form, equal and different.

So the Buddha liberated women. It's said that he always addressed his followers with something like "Men and women of good families," or maybe in correct English it would be "Ladies and gentlemen." It was probably highly unusual for any spiritual leader of his time to do this.

He ordained women, but not readily at first. He declined not because he considered them incapable but because he foresaw physical problems for women traveling around the countryside at that time in India. Because there were no established monasteries, there was no housing for monks. There were many practical reasons. Merely out of a desire to protect women and not to expose women to hardship, Buddha first took that position.

However, our beloved Ananda, his cousin, had a great heart for women. He saw the Buddha's foster mother and his wife appear with bloody feet and shaved heads having walked a great distance to join the Buddha and his sangha. After the Buddha had declined to ordain them, Ananda in his wisdom sought another approach. He asked the Buddha, "Venerable lord, are women capable of reaching Nirvana and arhatship?" And the Buddha said: "Yes, they are

---

"How do we get traditions? By breaking traditions."

---

capable of highest attainment." Then Ananda made a second request for ordaining women, and the Buddha admitted his foster mother and his wife as the first ordained nuns to the sangha.

He gave them a special set of rules which were based on the condition of the sangha at that time and place. It is said these rules were made for the protection of the men; not because Buddha thought the women were weak, but because men were weak. All the rules that evolved in Buddha's lifetime were not made by him when he first came out of his enlightenment. Later he said, "This human kind needs a set of rules to live by."

First he proclaimed the truth, the Dharma, the equality of all things, the impermanence of all things, and cause and effect. Then as they were living together as a sangha, being incompleted human beings, certain situations arose. So the rules and regulations that we have today for sangha were made at a specific time for specific circumstances. If you study Buddhism deeply, in the Prajna Paramita Sutra (the great Perfection of Wisdom Sutra which is one of the texts we study in the Zen tradition) you will find that the Buddha instructs his disciples (which he calls Bodhisattvas, Mahasattvas, the great enlightened beings, which is really every one of you, because you are on the same path whether you are aware of it or not), he instructs them this way: A Bodhisattva does not have the notion of a person or a being. A Bodhisattva does not take his stand on anything.

So what does this mean for us? We should not have the notion of a person, being a woman or a man. We should not take our stand on anything! That is the highest path, the path of transcendental wisdom. Of course, the Buddha also taught in accordance with the needs and realizations of individuals. We have many examples, parables, of how he taught. We also know that the Buddha did not only teach with words. He gave koans, a practice to do.

If you read sutras like the Diamond Sutra, you see that Buddha

Ruth Denison and Prabhasa Dharma

had a way of asking a question again and again. For instance in the Surangama Sutra, he asked Ananda, "Is the light of the lamp coming to your eye, or is your eye going to the light of the lamp? Is the sound of this bell going to your ears, or does your ear go to the sound?" If we want to know anything at all, we must go beyond the thing.

If we really want to know what Buddhism is for America, we have to sit down and forget both the old and the new. We all come, those of us who practice, from some tradition. And for the first time in the history of Buddhism, I think, we have all the Buddhist traditions in one country. In the United States we have the possibility of exploring and experiencing every tradition that has been developed in Buddhism—the Tibetan, the Chinese, the Korean, and so forth. If you don't have them here, come to Los Angeles! We have all of them.

That is also partly what is confusing to a lot of us, that we hear various interpretations. We see many different robes and hear chanting in many different languages. So we have to sit down and look at ourselves. When you are in one tradition, there is a tendency to think, "This is the way." This is one of the hindrances in this country, that on one hand we have all these traditions, which is a benefit and can be a great education, but on the other hand, there is a tendency among these teachers (which of course is their calling) to continue their lineage and their tradition. I understand this very deeply and was involved in it myself. I see their need to continue that lineage and tradition.

But what is tradition? How do we get tradition? By breaking traditions, right? Why do we have Rinzai Zen? Because Rinzai was different from Unmon and Joshu and other masters. They were flourishing schools of Zen and all established themselves as a tradition. When you look at how Buddhist monks dress, you can see that in every country they have evolved their own style of robe or interpretation of what the Buddha designated as the proper clothing for a monk. (Incidentally, when I say monk, I mean both male and female monks.) Therefore we must look at ourselves and see what is most appropriate for us.

In terms of women and society, when we look at history as a whole, I think more change has occurred in the last fifty years than in the 2500 before. I think the changes are more and more rapid. When I was a young art student, I always had a difficult time relating to ancient ways of painting, like the Venetian School or the Renaissance. I could see it, but somehow I did not feel very close to it. The same is true in religion. Religion that remains in the churches and the scriptures is useless, because it's dead.

We have to look at spirituality and the law of Manu that was for women in the Hindu world. Maybe some of the regulations that were made after the Buddha's death need to be investigated from the spiritual point of view, not from the letter but from the spirit of the law. The Buddha showed us the way. He really did not lay down anything. He did not even establish a monastery. At the end of his life he said, if you want to do that you can, but that was not my calling.

So each one of us is free to live the kind of life that we each want to make for ourselves. But freedom does not mean just willfully to do anything that comes into our minds. It is to be free from being stuck in the conditioned world, free to follow the Dharma, to be one with the Dharma. When the Buddha awakened from his great samadhi, he said, "Now I have found the deathless. I am the Dharma. When you see the Dharma, you see me. And when you see me, you see the Dharma."

It is my personal endeavor to live up to that as closely as I can. What that means in my life is to become transparent. There is no greater joy than to strip yourself of all the stuff, to take virtually everything off. You can only do that when you have realized that which is indestructible—your true nature. The true nature cannot be talked down or up, or destroyed or enhanced by anything. Therefore you can become vulnerable, because that which can be destroyed should go. That's what you want to get rid of, so let them take it.

I don't care what the Theravadan monks or the books say about women. I have to live my life in my own conscience, and that has to be aligned with the universe. That's the job I have to do in this life. That is my responsibility to myself, but in reality that means I am taking responsibility for all of you. That is the full meaning of the four Bodhisattva vows we chant. "I vow to save all sentient beings"— that is impossible if you look at it merely from the relative point of view.

When you realize yourself truly, you have realized all. Then you can stand up and say like Jesus said, "I am the Way. No one comes to truth but through me." That means the Dharma. The Buddha also said, "I am the Dharma. Between heaven and earth I am the only authority." Each one of you should get yourself in the position where you realize this and can manifest it in the world. Then we are free from notions of man and woman. We'll be humans that appear

---

"We are here in the world to play with the universe, to enjoy our true nature."

---

as male or female.

Language is a very important factor in our conditioning. I don't know where the English word "woman" comes from, maybe from "wooing man"? I don't know if there is another language where the word for woman or female contains a reference to man. There's usually a separate word for it. So you see perhaps the minds of Americans or English-speaking people are more conditioned, or are conditioned in a different way than in other countries.

I teach in Europe and part of my teaching is in German. I realized just recently when I give teishos on koans, that in English the koans are broken up into introduction, the case, the commentary and verse. The case in German is called *beispiel*. *Spiel* is to play, *bei* means next to or beside it. Also in German when we speak of living —*das leben spielt sich ab*—life plays itself off. There is always the word "play" in it.

Gesshin Prabhasa Dharma, Roshi

I had a great awakening in the middle of a talk and said to all these German people, "Do you realize you have forgotten how to play? Now life is a drudgery. You work hard and you have problems. A koan is like another play that runs alongside of my play. Here's another example, another play, is how we should preface all koans. Life is like this. We are here in the world to play with the universe, to enjoy our true nature."

When we enter Zen practice it seems in the beginning to be so difficult, particularly in my case when I trained with strong young men in the Rinzai tradition. For some masters that tradition has a lot of power and shouting and beating. That's the general impression people have of Rinzai tradition.

One of our major sesshins is Rohatsu in December, which is very severe with very little sleep and a lot of sitting. There were about fifty people in the zendo and I had practiced at that time maybe two to three years, when my master asked me to take the jikki jitsu position. I had done this many times before, but this was my first Rohatsu responsibility. I will never forget the first time I stood up from my seat, holding the kyosaku, the stick, in my hands and prepared to make my rounds through the zendo.

In the Rinzai monastery if there's the slightest move or even the sound of breathing, the jikki jitsu shouts. I reflected on myself. All my role models then were male, but I didn't feel like I could do that many times. It didn't feel right to me. It wasn't my nature. I didn't have the kind of musculature and bone and psychic structure that was required for that kind of action.

So what could I do? I was a woman. Was there any possibility in this for a woman? How would a woman do this? I didn't have any women to look at, so I had to look at myself.

While I was standing there I was totally helpless. Then it came to me. It is necessary to be firm and strong inside, but my nature is gentle and kind, so be both. Be gentle and kind on the outside but firm and strong inside, because you cannot let fifty people down on the third day when they all get crazy, confused, tired, or want to give up. You have to uphold them not with shouting around the zendo but with your own awareness and strength, your own spiritual strength and practice.

I'm telling you this because from then on I knew my way very clearly within my own limits. As a human being and a woman I have limits, and I have to work within them, because after all, the Dharma also manifests as the female as well as the male.

I would love to go more into this, but unfortunately our time is up. Thank you. ❏

Politics of the Heart

Jacqueline Mandell

It's a pleasure for me to be here, and I'm actually here as a woman. There are teachings and experiences transmitted through the Buddhist tradition that there's "no man and there's no woman." Thus, saying that "I'm a woman in the Buddhist tradition" is a bit "unkosher." Yet, it seems that now is a time when we actually can break down a lot of barriers which have inhibited us from looking at ourselves as women and as men.

When I first knew of the Women's Movement years ago, I wasn't interested. I chose not to involve myself in that movement even though I agreed with many of the ideals. I chose to follow the Buddhist path because it was the form of practice that I wanted.

Your invitation last year to speak here at the Providence Zen Center was one that sparked my inquiry into myself as a *Woman-*Buddhist teacher. It was my first time speaking at a women's conference. Upon reflection, I realized that as a teacher of Buddhism I represented a patriarchal form which held negative images about women. It was hard for me to come to terms with this because of what had been given to me by my teachers. They had given me guidance in a most open and generous way. I received the training openly along with my authorization to continue the delivery of these teachings. So my own step forward, which included my resignation from the Theravada tradition, came out of a "morality of responsibility."

I could no longer stand before women and say that I represent a tradition which does not recognize a woman as an equal being. In the Theravadan tradition, women are said to be a lesser birth. When women were accepted as nuns, Bhikkunis, they were asked to take eight rules which would make them subservient to men. These rules included: even a nun of the highest order had to bow down to a monk of one day; all nuns had to bow to monks, monks not to nuns; a monk may reprimand a nun, a nun may not reprimand a monk. And so forth.

There are traditions, not just Buddhist traditions but other religious, political-social systems which call themselves the "Truth." Yet within the embodiment of what they call the Truth, there are very political statements about men and about women.

It's possible to look at being a woman in a very new way. Many of the women leaders of the past were still under patriarchal obligations and patriarchal domination. It still may be that women leaders represent the patriarchy and have patriarchal conditioning. We see it in the business world, in the social and political world. Now we have women leaders going forth on their own without

---

"My own step forward, which included my resignation from the Theravadan tradition, came out of a morality of responsibility. I could no longer stand before women and say that I represent a tradition which does not recognize a woman as an equal being."

---

patriarchal constraints. This is very special. However, can women look at themselves as women? This is one of the challenges of our times.

There's a story in *Zen Flesh, Zen Bones* about a woman who made a decision to scorch her face in order to enter Zen practice. She was not accepted for Zen practice because she was too beautiful. This was "her problem." It was said that she would have distracted the monks from their practice. There's an article in the journal *Women and Religion*, called "An Image of Women in Old Buddhist Literature: The Daughters of Mara." In this article the Feminine is implicated as one of the last temptations of the Buddha. As he sat under the tree, Mara showed him images of beautiful dancing "ladies" to lure him away from enlightenment. Within

Buddhist traditions men and women have been separated, especially in celibate kinds of settings. One way of coping with these situations was to cast women in negative or problematic roles.

We must examine all of these images. This examining can take the form of a naming. It's not a naming to be held onto, but it's a naming to identify. In the latest book by Gloria Steinem, she talks about how there was never a name for "wife battering," it was just called Life! But now that there's a name there is more possibility of investigation and of solution. Don't be afraid to name or to identify. Learn to work with that. Certainly all of the traditions teach the nature of emptiness. We can also bring that wisdom into our noticing and naming. We can say for example, "Yes, there is wife battering"; "Yes, there are negative images of women in Buddhist texts. There are also some positive images." Looking at images and situations directly and naming them allows us to see them clearly.

I've heard too many distressing stories this year. Some of these have been published. Other stories I've heard directly from individuals. They included deep depressions of women students who were approached sexually by their teachers. The students did not know how to deal with this type of behavior. They had no context in their spiritual communities in which they could relate these kinds of experiences. At first there was little if any communication about these experiences. The most distressing story I heard was of a suicide. A woman had an affair with her teacher. Then, he left her and moved on to another place. This was too confusing for her.

Many of you have an enormous amount of life wisdom. You have seen a lot and have tried many things. You have tried to work on your problems and on your lives in many ways and you have come to spiritual practice. Then some of you, even with the life wisdom, turn away from looking at the current community problems, even to the extent of saying, "We don't have those problems here." Perhaps you think, " I just want to surrender, I don't want to think about that anymore." Here surrender is used as avoidance. A lot of you come here thinking, "That's not what I'm dealing with; I'm just dealing with meditation practice." And yet, we also have to remember our own maturity and adulthood.

There are certain phraseologies of becoming "Children of the Dharma," of having "child-like minds". This does not mean acting like a child. Some of you may not be able to look at these situations because of dependency. This could be dependency on the teacher or on the institution. This dependency needs to be looked at. I know this is a difficult investigation.

For myself, one step in assuming the investigation and the integrity of being a woman was to read many books by and about

Jacqueline Mandell and Jan Chozen Bays, Sensei

women. These books became a link to my intuitive and experiential understanding. I began my reading with women in Christianity and then with women in Judaism. They have looked at discrimination against women in religious institutions. I found a lot of information which related to what I was looking at. Then I went on to read books about women and patriarchy.

We are presented with all kinds of imagery from patriarchal religions. We may not know how great our conditioning is. There are patriarchal images of both men and women. In the Theravadan tradition, Buddhahood, the highest attainment of Buddhism, is not allowable for a woman. This might be the most discriminatory statement there is within that tradition.

Today one may actually be fulfilled in every way, as a woman or a man, not just a non-gender being. This includes fulfillment in your own spiritual practice to the highest degree. I am currently writing a book about women and spirituality. I want to share and to deepen this kind of inquiry which is so important for anyone interested in a clear perception of their spiritual growth. ❏

Inquiring Without Images

Toni Packer

I would like to make one correction about the introduction. It was mentioned that I was influenced by Krishnamurti. It is not a matter of influence at all, but simply a matter of seeing clearly for oneself, what is pointed out clearly. This is freedom from influence.

The title of this conference is "Women in American Buddhism." It is a fact that one is a woman or a man. Also that one has an image of oneself as a woman or a man. Not just one image but a whole host of images. That one is a Buddhist is an image. That one is an American is an image, apart from the fact that one carries some papers when one goes abroad. If one looks carefully, to think of oneself as American is tied up with images, emotions, and feelings of separation, as are all images.

Just before leaving to come here, I was asked a question by a woman who was working in the kitchen. (She had dropped in recently, and had been very active in women's movement.) She asked me, "What are you going to say to these people when you go? Are you just going to talk about this or that, or are you going to be concerned with women—how they have been downtrodden in spiritual traditions, placed at the bottom of the hierarchical structure? How men consider that women are incapable of liberation, emancipation, enlightenment (which holds for the Zen tradition as well as other Buddhist traditions)? There are women who are waiting to hear about it. Are you going to address yourself to this? What are you going to do about it?"

The work of questioning deeply into the human mind is more than specific issues or specific problems. The whole human condition is embraced. However, this work is not doing what we normally do and have been doing for hundreds and thousands of years: namely, rushing to solve problems in a more or less violent way. This work is to understand a problem, not just superficially, or even deeply, but totally. It is to understand so completely that the problem may be resolved not through a solution, but through understanding.

Before continuing, let me say something about listening— because we are from many different backgrounds, places, countries, traditions, or no tradition. How does one listen to a talk like this or the following ones? Can you listen carefully as though it was just a conversation between you and me? How are you listening? Do you have an image of Toni?

To my surprise, when meeting me, a lot of people say "I know about you. I've heard about you." So do you have an image? Knowing about Toni, having an idea about her, maybe you've read a little booklet, heard stories, and now you have an idea of what she

---

"Do you see that you do have an image of yourself as being somebody or many 'bodies'—being a Buddhist, being a woman, being an American?"

---

is or propagates. And do you have an image of yourself, what group or tradition you belong to? Is there the ever-readiness in the mind to compare what is being said to what one already knows? Then you're not listening. You're comparing, and what is really said flows by unheard.

So, at least for the short duration of this talk, is it possible to suspend what one knows, to suspend comparison? Can one just be open, completely open, not knowing how one will react, just receiving? If one has an image of oneself or of this person that is sitting here, this pure listening is impeded or distorted. One reads into it or subtracts from it, or one will not want to listen to some things at all. It may be too painful or too threatening.

Do you see that you do have an image of yourself as being somebody or many "bodies"; being a Buddhist, being a woman, being an American? The American image was recently very much appealed to by watching the Olympic games. Does one watch deeper than what one sees on the screen? When the national anthem is played, when the flags go up and our young men and women stand on top, does the patriotic heart start beating and feel good, having been given a boost—but a boost to what? A boost to an image! If one's country has won lots of medals, one doesn't mind seeing others win one too every once in a while, because one is also identified with the image of "brotherhood."

As far as one's religious affiliation is concerned, is one identified with it, attached to it, so that one's self-image includes and is invested in the religion, the religious group or center that one belongs to? This can easily be tested. When someone criticizes one's religion, does one feel defensive immediately, personally attacked and hurt? Or if somebody praises one's group or center, is one's vanity flattered? One's personal vanity, one's identification—this is "me".

And as a woman, what kind of images does one nurture, mostly unaware? Many people say to me that women have such a bad image of themselves, that one has to work on one's image, improve it, which means substituting a good image for a bad image. But why does one need *any* image? One doesn't understand the difficulties, the impediment, the separation that all images create within ourselves and among each other.

At times one may well have witnessed the battle of inner images: one wants to be a good mother, but one always wants to go to retreats. There are guilt feelings as the mother, and guilt feelings if one doesn't go to retreats enough. So there is a battle of images within, which expresses itself in general irritation. And in interpersonal relationships too there is strain; two people living together having images of themselves and the other inevitably creates contradictions. Who dominates whom? One feels manipulated and needs to manipulate because one has been manipulated.

Watch it for yourself. You will discover amazing things, what goes on in this mind and therefore throughout this body. Anything that goes on in this mind, any single thought, is totally connected with the whole organism—electrically, neurochemically. One pleasurable thought gives a gush of good feeling. Then one wants to keep that, which is another thought. "How can I keep that?" When it stops, "What have I done to lose it?" "How can I get it back?"

The poor body has to respond to all of this, not even done yet with the pleasure, when already there is pain. The body isn't done with it quickly. It takes the physical organism a while to get back into balance. I don't know whether our bodies even know what balance is anymore. There's so much residue still there, not just within the body, but of course within the brain.

We do all this mental bookkeeping, remembering what he or she did to us this morning, yesterday, a year ago, sometimes ten or fifteen years ago. "I'm not going to forget that," one says, which means no relationship with the person is possible. The person is branded, marked. One sees him or her and there is the image of what he or she did. Our response is dictated by the image, dominated by it. When there is an insight into this whole process, and one sees it, the seeing is already the interruption of it. Nonetheless, image-making may continue because it's very pleasurable to us. We live in and for our images, even if they're painful, because we think we have to live for something.

Can one question all this? I don't call this work "Zen" anymore, because the word is extra, unnecessary to the inquiry. This fundamental inquiry into the human mind and body (not *my* mind and body personally, but the human mind) doesn't need any descriptive label. To the extent that this mind (as it functions in images, in blockages, in contradiction and conflict) is clearly understood, the whole human mind is clearly understood, because it does not differ fundamentally from one person to another. On the surface, superficially, we're all different, but fundamentally each of us has an image of being a self, of being someone.

To see that this is an idea, a thought creation, seems inordinately difficult. The self-image feels so solid, so real, that one takes the self for a fact. One confuses it with this body and the ongoing processes of thought, sensations and emotion. But there is no owner of all this.

To say "this is me" and have an image—"*I'm* good at this, *I'm* poor at that"—is a mental construction, a bunch of thoughts and ideas just like any other thought and idea, part of that stream of thinking poured out by the brain. Yet "this is me" is the root of all our individual interpersonal problems and our international problems.

Most of you here are probable very concerned with the state of the world, the terrorism, the fighting that goes on in the Middle East and elsewhere. Recently I heard a famous news commentator, reporting about a new violent incident in Jerusalem where Christians, Muslims and Jews are at bloody loggerheads with each other.

"The self-image feels so solid, so real, that one takes the self for a fact. One confuses it with the body and the ongoing processes of thought, sensation and emotion. But there's no owner to all of this."

He said, "How is it possible, in the place where three of the greatest religions were born and all of them preach peace, that people kill each other? It's unfathomable." But if one thoroughly understands identification, investment, image, defensiveness, and aggressiveness by seeing it directly in oneself as it happens, then it is not unfathomable that members of religious groups fight each other and even kill each other.

So what is one going to do about all of this? Which was the question asked of me by this woman in the kitchen, "What are you going to do about it?"

It is a simple fact that this work can only start with oneself. If in oneself confusion reigns, images dominate and motivate one's action and position and goals of what one wants to be or to become —when *that* dominates the inner scene, how can one resolve confusion among each other and in the world? One just carries that confusion with one whatever one does. And yet will one start to look, to question everything, and leave no stone unturned, which may shake up one's whole foundation? One may anxiously or defiantly keep one's images and say, "I can't do without them, I'm attached to them. It's human nature."

But is one at least clear what one is doing? Can one see that one's foundation is one of separation and isolation, because it is divided from the foundations of other human beings? Each one is defending their own foundation. Believing in it, putting their refuge in it, and at times reaching as if over the foundation wall to shake hands with someone else, who reaches over his or her foundation wall to shake hands and to assure each other of mutual understanding—or can these walls break down completely? So that nothing separates us from one another? It is a tremendous challenge.

"It is a simple fact that this work can only start with oneself."

One may feel that I am exaggerating, that it's my opinion. I'm not trying to give opinions. I'm talking about what comes out of looking very seriously into oneself, and seeing the dangerous consequences of identification with something or somebody, and the danger of being somebody.

It's only when you really work on yourself, as many of you do, probing deeply and stopping nowhere—not "I'm only going this far and no farther"—but going all the way, that one really comes in touch with this fundamental anxiety of being nobody. And usually there's an immediate withdrawal from that anxiety. The human mind wants something to which it can cling. But will not one escape this time? Will you face the anxiety, just raw anxiety? Not stopping the questioning, but simply looking, feeling, listening, quietly with no goal in mind. Just being with what is there or isn't there in utter silence ...

Maybe there is a flash of insight into the fact that we are nobody, nothing. With this glimpse comes a joy that cannot possibly be put into words. It has nothing to do with words. It is no image, no thought.

Then the next moment, does one try to grab onto it, make it into an image? "I am somebody who has seen." "Now I know." Does one congratulate oneself again? Does one try to re-call and relive the experi-ence? Images come so quickly, like mushrooms springing out of the ground on a moist rainy day. There they are—new images. Will one see them immedi-ately and drop them instantly?

Or does one just carry on, "I've done this thing, I've gotten through it. This is it. I'm no one!" What does it mean— "I'm no one?" It's already become a concept, a memory.

So—is it possible to see and be free of images from moment to moment—really being no one and therefore completely open and related to everyone and everything, with a lovingness that cannot be produced through any kind of practice? Love is not practiceable. It's either there or it isn't, and it is *not* there when the "me" is there who wants to bring it about, who tries to grab it and hold on to it.

One may deceive oneself as being a loving kind of person, being very compassionate. Is it just an image? Do you see it when it comes up? Can it be dropped instantly so one really does not know what one is? Just letting action flow out of this not-knowing, just being in touch with what is within and before one—listening, seeing, responding openly? It's up to each one of us. No one can do it for us. Listen! ❑

Believing in Yourself

Barbara Rhodes, Ji Do Poep Sa Nim

It was wonderful for me to hear everyone share of themselves this weekend. It convinces me once again that we're all one big family. I hope we keep sharing our Dharma with each other. As has been mentioned already, there is a tendency for human beings to separate, to think "my practice is the best." We build walls, names and ideas. It's a human condition and it's very destructive. We are lucky in this country because we have this opportunity to share ideas. But we have to make an active effort or it's not going to happen. There's a pull toward separation all the time.

I was sitting in a sesshin with Sasaki Roshi last May. It was about the fourth day of the retreat. I was about to have my sixteenth interview. Things were so different from what I'm used to with Zen Master Seung Sahn. I had answered a couple of his questions, but there was one kong-an that I had been trying to answer for a day and a half and I kept thinking, "Where is my mistake?" All of a sudden a wave went through me, this wonderful feeling that I've had before many times. All of a sudden I had gotten it.

You have to believe in yourself. It's not so much that he was looking for a word, he was looking for a belief, a confidence to just have it come out ... believing in yourself. Then I went up and answered the kong-an. It was the same answer I had given two hours earlier. I just had confidence. I didn't care what he said. That is how I thought of the title for this talk.

The past several years many of the Zen centers in America have been having trouble. All of those things that we think of as hard times don't really have to be a hard time at all. All of those things are your teacher. Arrogance, laughing at someone, laziness are different traps. You say "thank-you" when anything appears. 1983, 1984, thank-you. All of the things that appear in this universe are for each one of us. Then there's no winning and no losing anymore. That's real freedom: freedom from life and death, from winning and losing, from pride and arrogance. Freedom from everything.

I led a retreat in Toronto last weekend. It was wonderful, nice weather, more people than usual, and everyone felt good. We always have a circle talk at the end and share something about the retreat. Several people told me they only see a teacher about every three or four months. They seemed hungry and grateful. You could say anything and they wanted to hear it. It's really easy, especially to say something nice. They almost draw it out of you. So three of the people who had been at the retreat took me to the airport the next morning. They said things like, "I can't wait until you come back," and "It was such a great retreat." They were full of admiration, and I saw the orange caution light appear.

"Good speech or bad speech, if either one touches you more than the other, you've got a problem."

That's dangerous, this attachment of people liking your teaching or needing and wanting you. It weighs exactly the same as someone saying "Thanks a lot, but I'd rather have so and so come up and teach. You weren't so great." Good speech or bad speech, if either one touches you more than the other, you've got problems: clinging, grabbing, not believing in yourself.

If you need good words to feel good about yourself, then it's devastating when someone gives you bad words. Neither one needs to touch you. At the same time, it's wonderful if someone tells you your teaching is inadequate and shallow. It's the same thing as "Wow, it's great, I can't wait until you come back!" Your mind doesn't need to move with either. You can feel a little sad about one reaction and a little proud or happy about the other, just happy that you make people happy. But then that feeling is gone and you're getting on the airplane, watching an old lady trying to pick up her heavy bag, helping her to carry it.

You're right there the next moment. I think that's the goods you get from sitting and practicing. That is Zen—being able to answer the next moment with no trace of the last.

I want to share one story that's been helpful to me. When Zen Master Seung Sahn, my teacher, had been in this country for six or eight months, everybody was always asking him questions about Korea, Buddhism, and enlightenment. Somebody asked him if there were any women Zen Masters in Korea. He said, "No, women can't get enlightenment."

Conference photographer Adeline Alex with Barbara Rhodes

I just looked at him. He gave these wonderful dharma talks about "don't make man, don't make woman, don't make anything." So I said, "Soen Sa Nim, you always say originally there is nothing. Don't make distinctions. Don't make good and bad or man and woman. What do you mean women can't get enlightenment?" I wasn't angry, I was just shocked that he was saying that. He looked at me and said, "So you're a woman!"

"I am a woman." "I am a man." Already enlightenment has passed through your fingers. It's not a thing. You can't get it. Nobody can get it. Buddha didn't get it either. So we don't have to worry. We're all in the same family and that's wonderful.

An eminent Zen teacher once said, picture yourself as an insect with sensitive antennae. How they stay alive and find their food depends on those antennae. To attain, or understand yourself, you can't let those antennae move at all, not one tiny vibration from either of them. They have to be completely still.

In a sense he's saying that any phenomenon appearing in our life makes us check or doubt ourselves or others by thinking and separating. If the antennae or the mind move just a fraction of an inch, you've already gone straight to hell. That's why enlightenment sounds so difficult. How could we ever be so clear that our minds don't move at all, that we can always just be there? The only time that the antenna is not moving at all is when you're meticulously paying attention to each moment.

So it's not the dishwater or the ninety-day retreat. Either one is food for our practice. One is not better than the other, although sometimes one is more supportive than the other. We have to become sensitive and balanced about those things and it's not easy.

Zen Master Seung Sahn once gave a talk at the end of our ninety-day winter Kyol Che retreat. He told about the high class Zen student, who only has to hear one word and he or she gets it. The second-class Zen student needs to sit a seven-day retreat and then gets it. The low-class Zen student has to sit ninety days and then gets it. So he asked, "Did you get it?"

Most of the people in the room began feeling horrible, doubting themselves, their practice. Then Zen Master Seung Sahn immediately said, just now, even this mind that doubts itself, this is enlightenment. It's "I didn't get it" enlightenment. He said it so compassionately and beautifully. It felt like he'd taken out a silver tray with twenty-five beautiful little cakes on it, one for each of the people in the room, their favorite flavor and color. Enlightenment cakes. I didn't get it, and that's it! Just believe in yourself, this mind this moment.

I really want to encourage people to find a teacher and a practice, anything that helps you practice consistently and to your fullest. It doesn't matter who the teacher is or what the form is. If you decide to get up in the morning and do 108 bows, to sit twenty minutes twice a day, or do a retreat twice a year, whatever it is, get yourself to do that.

We all have this resistance to practice. It's not an easy thing to practice hard. Sometimes we have to force ourselves to pay attention. We could be doing any kind of practice as long as it means mindfulness and consistency and accountability to someone. It's important to get some feedback about your practice once in a while.

There's a story that goes with that. Up in the seventh heaven, the King of Kings of all the heavens and the universe was sitting on his throne, feeling tired and old and thinking it was time to pass on his

responsibilities. He looked at his attendant and said, "I want to find a person to replace me: the perfect compassionate, all-knowing person. I'm ready to retire."

The attendant said, "How can we find this being?" The King of Kings said, "Don't worry. There's a certain fellow that I've had my eye on." It was Shakyamuni Buddha, in one of his previous incarnations.

So the King of Kings went flying down over the different realms and found the Buddha in a cave. The King manifested himself as a hawk, and had his attendant manifest himself as a dove. The hawk soared around and made threatening moves toward the dove, right over the Buddha's head.

The Buddha looked up, very compassionate and loving, and saw the dove's predicament. He yelled up to the hawk, "Please don't attack that dove. Don't eat it!" The hawk said, "Why not? I'm hungry."

Buddha replied, "Oh, the dove will suffer so much! Please don't kill him." But the hawk said, "I'M HUNGRY!"

So Buddha said, "You may have one of my fingers to eat." The hawk produced a scale and put the dove on one side of the scale, which dipped way down. Then he said, "Give me an equal amount of meat and I won't eat the dove."

So the Buddha chopped off his hand and put it on the scale. The

---

"That is Zen—being able to answer the next moment with no trace of the last."

---

scale barely moved. The dove was much heavier. Then the Buddha cut off his forearm and put that on the scale, but the dove was still much heavier. He continued to dismember himself to try to equal the weight of the dove, but everything he offered didn't weigh enough.

This great question of how much can I give, how hard should I practice, appears when our practice is genuine. In this story we're racing through Buddha's mind, the great caring mind of "what can I do?" until finally he gets it. Because he had a strong question and a strong direction, he got it. He put his whole self on the scale and then it was much heavier than the dove. Then of course the hawk manifested himself as the King of Kings, and the Buddha became whole again.

This is a very lofty old story. We tend to think we couldn't be that compassionate. But that's our situation at the moment, seeing other beings in distress. Because we're not sensitive enough, most of the time we don't even see that distress, or sense the sadness that is going on around us. The longer we practice, the more we begin to see the suffering of others as well as our own suffering and faults.

It's at this point that a lot of people draw away from practicing. As you become more aware and sensitive, you think you're worse than you were five years ago, but you're not.

The day after my Toronto retreat where I had been so "wonderful," I was at work and I couldn't get one of my patients to swallow her medication. I was very tired and eventually lost my temper, and had to get one of the aides to give the pill. Walking down the hall I could see my frustration, my lazy karma, my laziness enlightenment. Zen Master Seung Sahn would call that "losing it" enlightenment.

If you can't see that in yourself, you can't teach anybody else. You can't share or be anybody else's friend unless you see those things in yourself. So when you are losing your temper, take a good look at it. The next time you see someone else acting that way, there's no separation—you have complete understanding and maybe you can give that person support. That's our job.

So they loved me in Toronto and the next evening I'm an impatient, weary nurse. Which one is correct? KATZ! I hope we all learn to believe in ourselves and help others. ❏

Taking Realization Into Everyday Life

Jan Chozen Bays, Sensei

I want to express my gratitude for all the teachers, students, and Dharma friends over all the generations whose practice brought us here today. We all have areas of clarity and unclarity. If we can meet together like this, we can share those areas and help each other. We are all together in the same search: to find out who we are, what our life is about, to find some measure of contentment no matter what life brings us.

The form of that search may be very different. We may be Sufis or Rajneesh followers or Buddhists. We may dress in red or purple, black or brown. I think one of the chief dangers is to feel, "My way is right." We always want confirmation by having people join our way or our group. For this generation I feel we must be beyond that. We must be able to talk to each other and share our areas of clarity and unclarity.

It's very easy to say that spiritual people are better than non-spiritual people, or Zen Buddhism is better than Mahayana or Hinayana or Tibetan Buddhism. That comparison and judging goes on endlessly. To drop that is one of the fundamental teachings of our practice.

Once the search begins it never seems to stop. Wherever we are, we're looking for clues. We read books, listen to Toni, Maurine, Gesshin, and Jacqueline. Some part of us is always looking for answers. When we start to practice, the differences disappear. We sit together in uniforms, in uniform rows, with uniform hair, schedule, and chanting. This is a very important step in trying to put down the separation, the small-self-ego that causes our distress and conflicts. We are trying to realize oneness. But as we practice, differences arise.

I've heard women talking about the problems they have in practice, problems I do not often hear from men, even though men and women are sharing jobs more now. If we are working women with households, children, a spouse or partner, and on top of that we have practice, then our days are more than full. We wake up in the morning and first thing, we go over lists. The day goes by too fast. As we go to bed at night, we wish we had at least six more hours.

We pick up lint as we cross the room. As we turn out the light, our last vision is of the kitchen floor that needs washing. "Oh well, tomorrow I'll sit." Just no time to do it all. Our days are so full, we wash the diapers in the toilet bowl, thinking, "I know this is practice, too, but I *really* want to be in the *zendo*."

Meditation is such a relief, to have a few moments to ourselves.

"We picture our child wandering through the neighborhood dirty in an unironed shirt, thumb in his mouth. Someone says, 'Where's your mommy?' 'My mommy is getting enlightened.'"

The place I use to have for these moments to myself was, and still is, the bathroom. I can sit in the bathroom for ten whole minutes of solitude. But usually there is a child lying against the door sobbing, "Mommy, when are you going to come out here? Are you going number one or number two?"

When we start to practice, we discover how wonderful those moments are, to stand back, reflect on our lives, order our priorities, have the chaos settle down, and become calm enough to go back into the fray. When we get a little taste of that, we want more.

The spiritual hunger is tremendous. The spiritual thirst is tremendous. We are almost afraid to open the door because when it opens, it opens wide. We have a tremendous yearning to take the search all the way to the bottom, to put aside all the things that restrict and bind us and keep us from pursuing that search full-time.

To do that, we have to do zazen. We have to do retreats, set aside hours, days, weeks to pursue that search. Meanwhile, what are we leaving at home? Jobs, housework, children. As we sit, visions of spiritual orphans float through our heads. We picture our child wandering through the neighborhood, dirty in an unironed shirt, thumb in his mouth. Someone says, "Where's your mommy?" "My mommy is getting enlightened."

A real conflict arises. We cannot ignore it or push it all down. Even when we have the best kids in the world, the most supportive spouse, the best child care, still these problems arise. We feel divided. The more our spiritual thirst grows, the more we feel divided.

We might imagine giving voice to these various elements in us (Toni calls them images). There is a powerful monastic element in each of us, and if we could give that full voice, it might say, "I don't want to wait until I've raised children and grandchildren—like that lady I heard about in Japan who entered the monastery at 83. I don't want to waste my time by night or day. I want to be like the Buddha. I want to clear the way and leave behind all the obstacles and restrictions. I want to practice full time. Before I die, I *have* to see it through to the bottom. If my spouse doesn't follow me, then he has his own work."

That's the monastic voice speaking, purely and strongly. We have other voices. Another might say, "Are you kidding? Practice is real life. You can't go and sit in the zendo all day long. You have kids at home, and housework to do. What good is it to meditate for the weekend? Two hours later when you get home, you're yelling at the kids? That's practice? That's escape. Your practice is your everyday life. You sit in the zendo and you're thinking about cooking and cleaning. When you're cooking and cleaning you're thinking about sitting in the zendo. That's crazy."

Then there are other voices. There's one that says, "I love being married. I love waking up in the middle of the night and feeling that warm body next to mine. If I have a nightmare, someone takes me in his arms. I love being pregnant, the magic of having new life inside. I love nursing a baby at the breast. I love seeing my kid off to school on the first day all dressed up and carrying a lunch box, going off to a new world, or a teenager learning to drive the car. I even love soapy dish water and my dirty kitchen floor. I love it all."

All these parts are the Buddha nature. We try to say, "No, I want to be in the zendo, not diapers now. I will be spiritual, not worldly." Conflicts and suffering come from trying to cut a part out, or attaching to it. In spiritual practice you often see people saying or feeling that there's a spiritual way to be. You might think that you're supposed to be even-tempered. You could even practice it in front of the mirror. "What, me angry? No, I don't get angry, I love everyone." It's a mask over what's really there. What's there is there. No one thing is more Buddha than any other thing. Everything is the Buddha, the enlightened way.

You can't throw part of the Buddha out. You can't cut off his hand and throw it out. We try to do it because we have ideas of how things should and shouldn't be. But all these things are parts of our Buddha self.

We also have a no-self, because the parts are constantly changing. The mother part, the part that likes housework and the part that doesn't, the part that likes to sit, all these parts come and go. They are constantly changing, EMPTY. All of these parts are us, and all are not us. Call them the relative and the absolute. What does that really mean in my life?

Relative means that I am all of these parts. None can be denied. The absolute means that none of the parts are me. Constantly shifting, we can't hold on to them or exclude any of them.

Recently a student who is a Christian and a Zen student came to me. She had just joined an Episcopal church. There was a confirmation class with the pastor who presented the Apostle's Creed. She demanded that he go over it with her because there were parts of it she agreed with and parts that she didn't agree with. She went through it line by line with him saying, "Yes, maybe that one. No on that one, but maybe I'll think about it." That's who we are, parts that come and go. Today it's "no, not that part; maybe tomorrow." But the very part that we don't allow in ourselves is what causes trouble eventually, both inside and outside.

The part that we have not recognized or not experienced "inside" is easy to recognize "outside," because we have that extra negative energy about it. As Christ said, it's easier to see the mote in someone else's eye than the log in our own eye. "I really don't like that person." That person is our teacher, a good koan.

What is there in that person that we're not allowing in ourselves? For example, there are the terrible realities of child abuse and wife beating. The problem is not the wife-beater out there. It's the wife-beater in here, the part of us that says, "You stupid wife! The house isn't clean, it's six o'clock, he's going to come home tired in ten minutes. You don't have dinner organized, and the kid's room is a mess." You see? That's the wife beater in us.

There's a spiritual beater in us too. We all know the part that says, "I'm not doing it well enough." C.S. Lewis, the British author, wrote "Surprised by Joy," a story about his leaving Christianity as a child and coming back to it as an adult.

He remembered a time in his childhood when he was told to say prayers and be attentive to *every* word. He would kneel on the cold hard floor by his bed at night and say his prayers. When he got to the end he would wonder if he had been attentive to every word. Then he would start again at the beginning and go all the way through them again, and again. He said he spent hours as a ten-year old child on the floor at night, trying to pay attention to every word of his prayers. The energy he put in was the energy that drove him away from spiritual practice.

"No one thing is more Buddha than any other thing."

We have that energy too, that says, "You must do it right. You're not doing it well enough." It's a ferocious energy, the same wonderful energy that keeps us trying. It's the part that gets up at 4:45 in the morning to do 108 bows. Halfway through the bows another part comes up and says, "Are we up to fifty yet? I sure hope somebody is counting!"

The very part that we don't recognize in ourselves is the part that will give us trouble. Our practice is to become wider and bigger, to encompass more energies, more ways of living, more images. Whenever we see ourselves resisting, angry, unhappy, there's the place to go. There's the bowing mat.

Then the other part of our problem appears. We don't recognize the emptiness. We don't recognize what is constantly changing. We try to fix it or hold it in some way. "Oh! I am a vegetarian meditator. This will always be my life." Right away we're headed for trouble. The fundamental teaching of the Buddha is impermanence, constant change. We have to recognize that we are all of it, and it is constantly changing. Emptiness is not like some big black void waiting for us to fall into it and yell for help. Emptiness is constant change, nothing fixed, nothing permanent.

We are a celibate nun, and also we're very sensual people who love being married and having relationships. We are very vulnerable and frightened and childlike, and also very clear-minded and steady, with diamond-like wisdom to cut aside any impediment. We are also fluffy-brained and confused and forget things. We're health food nuts who love to eat burned oatmeal in the morning because "It's good for our practice." We also love those Pepperidge Farm cookies with the sugar icing for tea break.

We are vegetarians and meat eaters. If we don't recognize the meat-eater in us we cannot relate to them "outside". A whole world is off-limits to us. Right away there are conflicts. "You guys are not on the right path, I am." It doesn't mean we have to eat meat, but, being both carnivores and vegetarians, we can choose freely each moment which to be.

There are endless ways to divide us up into little boxes and say "This is the right box." *All* those parts constantly changing and flowing are us. If we try to exclude a part, it's going to cause us trouble.

As a pediatrician I talk to many parents. I have to know there's a child-abuser in myself, or I can't work at all with child-abusers. If I don't know that part of me, boy, they know it right away: "Here comes that goody-goody." We all have parts that come home frazzled after a hard day's work and haven't sat a sesshin in two months because our husband got to do the sesshin this time, and when the kid starts crying and whining, you want to open the window and throw him out. Or you want to say to your teenager, "Look, see you later when you get your act together. Come back in about five years."

Knowing and exploring all those parts is exploring Buddha nature. It's not just human nature, it's everything. I am the grass, the leaves, the Datsun Z. I am Ronald Reagan.

I am a star and a piece of dirt. All of that blending together and constantly changing is who we are. It's not a blend in the sense of gruel, like on the seventh day of sesshin when the cooks keep mixing the leftovers from days before into the pot and it comes out all gray with some little green flecks in it, not tasting like anything. It's a rich and lovely blending like Chinese food, that preserves and recognizes the diverse elements: salty, sweet, spicy, crisp and soft, and so on. That's what our mixture is—delicious. Our Buddha nature is delicious, as Gesshin said.

We mentioned the notion that women don't have Buddha nature or can't become enlightened until they become men. Should we reject that notion? Or can we examine it, ask what it means in a deeper sense ... women can't become enlightened until they are born as men? Absolutely right! I can't become enlightened until I have been born as a *man*, as a *woman*, as *neither* and as *both*.

Men cannot become enlightened until they know their masculine nature, their feminine nature, the nature that is neither and both.

So let us practice together. Every life and every minute of life is communion, coming into union with who we are. ❏

Panel Discussion

Saturday, September 15, 1984

Suzanne Bowman, Director of the Providence Zen Center, introduced the five speakers and acted as moderator. On the panel were Gesshin Prabhasa Dharma, Roshi; Maurine Stuart, Roshi; Barbara Rhodes, Ji Do Poep Sa Nim; Jacqueline Mandell; and Jan Chozen Bays, Sensei.

Question: I would like to hear each of the teachers say something about Zen in America.

Prabhasa Dharma: I don't teach Zen in America. *(laughter)* I was going to say, this is it. We are all "it," you know. Without us, there is nothing in America. But I could add to that. A few years ago, I was on television in Austria with several nuns, one of them Theravadan. In Austria, Buddhism was not recognized as a religion, therefore the Buddhist Union in Austria could not establish itself as a religious organization and had to be registered as a club. They hired a lawyer and pursued the matter, which took about four years. Austria is largely a Catholic country, and religion and government are closely related.

The TV interviewer asked, "When could it be said that Buddhism has taken root in Austria? What do you think?" The Theravadan nun answered, "When there is a monastery and Buddhist monks can live and train there, one could say that Buddhism has come to Austria."

When the question came to me, I looked straight into the camera and said, "You don't have to worry, it will never come here, because it isn't something you can import or export. In fact, it is everywhere."

Barbara Rhodes: I think of Zen as being the desire to understand yourself, so it is not limited to Buddhism. Even people that claim to be agnostic or atheistic aren't, because they care. To me, Zen has always been in America, more than 200 years.

Question: My question is primarily addressed to Jacqueline and Maurine. This morning when you spoke, Jacqueline, you said that one of the reasons you had left Insight Meditation Society and stopped representing Theravadan Buddhism was because women were not able to attain Buddhahood in that tradition. Later in Maurine's group, she said that was not her understanding of how it works. I was left a little confused. It feels like an important issue to me, about the status of women in the practice.

"When we look into one another's eyes and the life in the place is lightening up and everybody feels something wonderful happening here, this is Buddha."

Jacqueline Mandell: I'll start with my own training. First of all, that was not one of my key reasons for leaving, but I did include it as a point to be considered. In India and Southeast Asia, the notion that women cannot attain Buddhahood is common knowledge. For references, see my book list *[published in the back of this book]* of women in Buddhism. This point is discussed in an article by Nancy Faulk entitled "Daughters of Mara" in the book *Women and Religion* edited by Judith Plaskow. This is common knowledge in both Theravadan and Tibetan Buddhism and it's in the Abhidharma *[early Pali texts in the Theravadan tradition that are thought to be the original words of the Buddha]*. One of the key reasons is that there are supposedly thirteen marks or characteristics of the body of one who becomes a Buddha, and one of them is having "a penis in a sheath".

Maurine Stuart: I don't have any particular reference to cite, except that I've been taught that every sentient being has Buddha nature. I feel that includes me. Buddha did not write any of these things. It was monks and other people who wrote these things down and made up these little rules and regulations. They were part of a particular culture, a time and a place which is not ours. My teaching and tradition has encouraged me to feel that I have every right to feel that I am Buddha, you are Buddha, everybody is Buddha from the beginning, without exception. Soen Roshi always said, "Without exception, every single one of us is Buddha."

I don't have any texts to offer you, any books to say on what page it says this. I only feel very strongly that Buddhahood is something in each one of us. When we look into one another's eyes and the life in the place is lightening up and everybody feels something

---

"Zen will never come to America, because it isn't something you can import or export. It is everywhere."

---

wonderful happening, this is Buddha. That is my feeling, my answer, not based on any book but on my living experience with my Zen teachers, living dynamic experience which I feel here with you.

Prabhasa Dharma: We have to make it clear first that Zen does not depend on any scriptures. Bodhidharma *[the First Patriarch of Zen]* said that Zen is a teaching independent of levels and scriptures. It is a direct pointing at man's heart, and thereby awakens his Buddha nature. The Buddha himself on his deathbed said that you should rely only on the light within yourself. He commanded us to throw away even his own teachings, to look at them as a raft that merely carries us to the other shore. What human being would carry a raft on his back after he has reached the other shore and is safely on land?

From the very beginning there is nothing, and that nothing we call Buddha or God or whatever, when we give it a name. Naturally it is all, total, absolute, all inclusive. But human beings, in their relative world and with their incomplete consciousness, started to write these things down after Buddha's death. I have personally investigated this matter by way of meditation, and I don't think the Buddha could have said anything that would have been discriminatory against women. Even in the Pali scripture *[early Indian Buddhist texts]* you can find that he said there should be no discrimination based on nationality, race, or creed. He never mentioned the sexes, because he was one who liberated women in his time.

I'm sure if the Buddha lived here today he would make a different set of rules, for example, about clothing. In those days in India, the monks were allowed to wear a certain number of wraps of cloth. That was appropriate for India, the Buddha himself tried out what was needed for that climate. But if he lived in Siberia today, I'm sure he would designate different kinds of clothes.

He encouraged us to investigate, always to investigate in our own mind and heart what is appropriate, and that can be done by way of meditation, by transcending the relative and getting a fresh look at things as they are and where they are at this time. This is what I

Barbara Rhodes, JDPSN; Gesshin Prabhasa Dharma, Roshi; and Jacqueline Mandell.

practice. I've come to my own insights.

In the Diamond Sutra, a Mahayana text taken from the larger Prajnaparamita Sutra (and tonight we chanted the Heart Sutra, which is a further condensation of this text) for example, when the Buddha is asked by his disciples, "Can the Tathagata be recognized by marks or signs?" he said no. "There are no marks, no signs. One who is looking for the Buddha by marks or signs is on the wrong path. If you adhere to my voice or my body or to any marks or signs, that is not the true Tathagata. This is not the Buddha." So that is the scriptural support for my point, but basically Zen practitioners don't rely on the scriptures, because they are unreliable. We should rely on our own insight.

Question: I wonder if the teachers could comment on the evolution of and/or monastic practice for women.

Barbara Rhodes: I haven't had any monastic experience. My school *[the Kwan Um School of Zen]* has had maybe ten or twelve ordained, celibate monks in the Korean tradition. About half of them have left. So we built a temple. Because you have a special life and special rules that you live by when you become a monk, you need special accomodations which have not been offered before by our school. Hopefully this temple will be more supportive for the monks. In our school, female monks also have to be celibate and have shaved heads, they can't wear wigs. Zen Master Seung Sahn has said, "If you do it, then do it completely."

Before I got married, I was thinking about becoming a monk. I asked Zen Master Seung Sahn if I could wear a wig just to work, because I loved my job and the Zen Center needed the money. He said no. As a result, I felt it was not a practical or necessary move for me. Having a shaved head is a big issue for most women in our school. It's such a major change and at this point there are not really good support systems for it. They will have to be developed.

Jan Chozen Bays: I think we are very much in evolution in the

United States. At the Zen Center in Los Angeles, at first, only men were ordained. One woman, who was single, was ordained later and she left about two years after that. A number of the ordained men were married. In Japan in my tradition *[the Soto tradition]* ordained men can be married, but ordained women are not allowed to be married. The reasons are partly historical.

About two hundred years ago the government of Japan became worried about the amount of land, power, and money held by male monks and monasteries. So at one point the monks were required to marry. The feeling was that marriage would dilute their energy and their land holdings would be divided up among their sons, and so forth. So there was a time in Japanese history when many monks were married, either above-board or secretly. When my teacher *[Maezumi Roshi]* came to this country with that tradition, he was faced at our Zen Center with many women who wanted to become ordained.

"There is a monastic element in all of us. The question is, how should we honor that?"

Most of the women remained shaved, or shaved at various points in their training, but it's very awkward to work outside the Zen community and have children, and be shaved. I've tried all the variations of wigs, scarves and a little bit of hair—it's quite awkward. With each thing I've tried, I've gotten a different reception. When my hair was less than an inch long, I tried to go out and work in the world as a physician. *[Jan is a pediatrician.]* At one medical conference, all I got was pitying looks. You know, "Poor thing, she's on chemotherapy ..." When I wore a scarf, like a modified Catholic nun's scarf, then doors were opened for me, I was shown to chairs, and it was "Sister, sister" all over the place. Nothing seemed right. So I think we are in a period of transition.

I don't want to give away my talk *[scheduled for the next day]*, but one thing I want to say is that there is a monastic element in all of us. That was said at the international conference on monasticism, the one at which Thomas Merton met his death. The question is, how to honor that monastic element in ourselves? Also, to what degree should we honor that—by becoming fully ordained as celibate monks or nuns and by living that life, or by living some intermediate kind of monastic life, like the Bodhisattva monks here *[at the Providence Zen Center]*, or like the monks and nuns at ZCLA? There we really aren't monks and nuns, we're trying to call ourselves "priests," but that doesn't quite work either.

Or should we live like a lay person who occasionally goes into retreat, and recognizes the monastic element that way? In many Southeast Asian countries, for instance Thailand, many lay people have a period in which they're ordained—it could be a month, or three months. All the kings of Thailand are ordained. In fact, when his brother died, the king was called out of perhaps twenty years of monastic life and inherited his brother's harem of about twenty wives! He went from one extreme to the other.

Prabhasa Dharma: He should have ordained them all. *(laughter)*

Jan Chozen Bays: Whether we'll develop something like that, where people can move in and out of ordination depending on their life circumstances, I don't know. We're very much in transition. It's very awkward to call ourselves monks and nuns and have children running up and saying "Mommy" and "Daddy" when you're talking to Catholic monks and nuns as equals.

Jacqueline Mandell: I had temporary ordination in Thailand. I was a temporary nun in Burma and again in California with a Burmese forest monk. I wore robes and a shaved head and took vows. It was quite extraordinary in that it felt like a change. Something was required that was obviously more than physical. At the same time, I realized that wasn't my life's path. Personally I haven't looked into what monasticism might evolve into in this country, but I do know it was a wonderful experience for me.

Prabhasa Dharma: Just a few weeks ago I was in Sri Lanka at the Buddhist World Conference. It was an interesting experience, because I was the only ordained woman in a delegate position. And it was also a "delicate" position, because in a Theravadan country where the nuns are not recognized as an existing order *[because of disruptions in the lineage]*, there were 2500 or 3000 nuns. Therefore a lot of questions were put to me and it made me look at a lot of things I don't usually have time to look at because I'm busy travelling and keeping my retreats going.

One of the things I've noticed here tonight is that when we are talking, we make so many assumptions. For instance, the question about what is Zen in America—we make the assumption we know what Zen is. It's a vast question and we really have to investigate much more. So when we talk about nuns and monks, there are many different experiences of that. Even though I was also trained by a Japanese master, my experience is quite different from that of Jan Chozen's.

When I shaved my head, my master bought me a wig because he

didn't want to be seen with me with my shaved head when we were travelling. Everybody stared at us in planes and trains. I never wore that wig because I felt like a monkey. *(laughter)* I have a small head anyway and it was the smallest wig I could get that still came down over my ears, and I put it back in the bag and took it back to the store that same afternoon. *(more laughter)* My master had gone to that store with me personally and bought that wig—it was honey blond and he said it looked gorgeous on me. So that was just the opposite experience from Jan Chozen's.

When I was in Japan training I had some association with nuns from other Buddhist sects, from the Jodo tradition. I asked them why, particularly in the Jodo tradition, there are no monks? There are priests and they have hair and marry and live a householder's life, but the nuns must be celibate, shave their heads, go to a nun's school and are actually trained and ordained as nuns. I asked one progressive and highly educated nun, "Why do you allow this? Why don't you have the same rights as men?" And she said, "Because we don't want them. This is our way."

This is not the only nun I talked to who felt that way; there were several others. And this was the way in which women could liberate themselves, could have time and space and support to pursue their spiritual life. In that society, the women have maintained this position because it keeps their possibilities to pursue a life of spiritual practice and study. Otherwise, if they married and had families, they were expected to stay home and take care of the house and raise the children, whereas the men were free to go out and pursue their careers. In that country, it worked out in that particular way.

It also depends on what kind of vows you take. In Japan, nuns and monks take ten precepts, whereas in other countries, a fully ordained nun or monk takes hundreds of vows and both nuns and monks are celibate and cannot marry. So we have to know more of the details. It's not enough just using the title "nun" or "monk."

I have never trained with women, with nuns. Both in this country and in Japan, I always trained with men. I had the special situation of being allowed to practice in a monastery with men, except for at night when they slept in the zendo and I had my own private room, and a bath which I could not share with them. So my training was entirely with men and under men, all the time, and I had no idea what a nun's training was like ...

You have to go back to zero, look at your situation in your particular community, and see how you can work it out, based on principles that you have realized through meditation.

Moderator: On that note, we need to hold our universe together with some emptiness. We said we'd sit at this time and I think that would be the most fruitful thing we can do together. Thank you very much. ❏

The 1985 Conference:

*The Balancing of
American Buddhism*

Obstacles as Our Teachers

Bhikshuni Ane Pema Chödron

I'd like to talk about the notion that obstacles can be our teachers. First, I want to discuss the whole logic of precepts in terms of relating to obstacles. Precepts have to do with simplifying. It's like having a large white canvas. Because it is so simple, you notice when even the tiniest speck of dust lands on it. You take a ballpoint pen and make a tiny dot and everyone can see it, as opposed to the usual situation of a canvas with a lot going on. On a busy canvas. you couldn't find that dot if you searched with a magnifying glass for a long time. Simplifying has a lot of power to teach you about yourself.

The whole notion of obstacles is just from our point of feeling that we've been intruded upon. Nevertheless, it causes a great deal of pain. We can feel like we're wearing dark glasses, ear muffs, layers of mittens and boots and that we don't experience our existence at all. The obstacle creates in all of us here, and in many people in the world, a great longing to figure out how to be free of that sense of separateness. You want to hear the birds singing, to taste your coffee. You want to feel fully alive and you aren't, so you call that "obstacle."

From the point of view of anyone who's pretty well or completely woken up, there really aren't any obstacles. When you look out of your eyes at the world, it seems rugged and smooth, bitter and sweet, hard and soft, fiery and cool, but you don't consider that a problem, but as reality. Precepts is like ground logic and it pervades the mind of meditation. It's the logic of simplifying things down to a point where you can see clearly, and allowing a lot of space so that insight or self-awareness can occur. If there's silence, you hear the birds.

The interesting thing is that even if there's a silence, sometimes

Precepts
To
simplify!!

you still don't hear the birds, because there's so much noise in your head. From the very compassionate and wise viewpoint of the Dharma, the way to work with an obstacle is not the way we usually proceed: "I hate this situation! I wish it would go away. If it weren't for my mind, my meditation would be perfect. If I jog every morning, I will be better than I am now. If I meditate well, I will be better than I am now."

This is a subtly aggressive attitude toward ourselves and reality. From the compassionate and intelligent viewpoint of the Dharma, to work with an obstacle is to become intimate with it. You can't get rid of ego, you look at it. You become very intimate with yourself and your world, but it begins with your own mind. So the logic of precepts is to simplify things.

Traditionally, this is referred to as "refraining from causing harm" or "refraining from continuing the chain reaction." Precepts

---

"Things get very clear when you're cornered."

---

acknowledge that all kinds of things occur in the mind. For example, you would like to punch that person right in the nose. You would really like to gossip and slander them, or post their name on a list in the hallway. You would like to harm them through your actions and speech. Everyone has these feelings.

This basic logic, the ground of discovery or of being truly inquisitive, is to simplify things so that you can see what occurs in your mind. The trick is to see it as a pathway towards developing loving-kindness towards yourself and others, rather than as a pathway to self-denigration. Meditation is very helpful. But precepts have to do with either ceasing to cause harm through your actions or through speech. They are considered broken only by the act of breaking them. You don't break the precept of lying unless somebody believes you. You don't break the precept of killing unless you really wanted to kill and the being is dead. The same is true of the precepts about sexual misconduct, drinking, stealing and drug abuse.

Begin With Not Harming

The way I have been taught about precepts is to begin with simply not harming. This goes a long way toward reducing chaos in your life and in the lives of others. Things are a lot simpler if you don't punch the guy in the nose, because punching him starts off a whole chain reaction of emotional upheaval on everyone's part, as we all know.

Maybe you're a person who has punched others quite often. It's an habitual pattern. You grew up in a family where everyone punched. To keep the precept, you feel as if you would have to tie

---

"What I have been taught about precepts is, begin with simply not harming."

---

your hands down, because punching is so habitual. The point is, you learn a lot from the arising of the impulse, from the longing to complete that act. What is it that comes up in you that makes you want to act? Insight or self-discovery is actually the whole idea.

There's another important point in precepts, about authority figures. No one tells you that you have to do this. In fact the whole logic of monasticism is that more than anything , you want to find out how it is that you keep yourself deaf and dumb, how you keep circling around the same old things year after year. In the process, you don't discover exactly how, but you become so familiar with yourself that the insight itself is what brings freedom and opening and softening.

The important thing is that no one tells you that you have to do this. Keeping precepts comes from a real desire to know. Meditation can also be looked at in this way, like a mirror. It's as if someone videotaped you all day long and at night you had to sit down and look at yourself. Meditation is your most compassionate and loving friend, rather than your critic. There's no way for human evolution to flourish and go forward into the unknown, without people becoming very familiar, in an unjudging way, with how things are in the moment.

Usually the kind of "do not's" of the precepts—do not steal, do not kill, do not lie, do not have sex, do not drink—sound like your parent putting candy on the table and saying "Don't eat it." You long to eat it. It seems right to eat it. And as soon as the parent goes away, you do eat it. It's like a big lid put on top of you that just makes you mischievous and resentful.

Poison On The Table

Precepts is actually like someone putting poison on the table and saying, "Don't eat it." You wish to find out how to not eat it, because if you do eat it, you will suffer. You might actually eat it,

hopefully only a little, in order to discover that it is poison. But the whole idea is, that it is poison which causes suffering to you and therefore you want to find out how not to perpetuate suffering for yourself and others.

That's the precept logic: wanting to know. The result is simplifying and some kind of tamed quality or personal harmony which is based on coming up against all one's sharp points. But if you limit your activity, you don't immediately plunge into tranquility. In fact, you begin to come up against all those yearnings to act out. This can be very uncomfortable, but you begin to want to experience the discomfort just so that you will understand. Then as you come up against one sharp point after another, you don't consider it bad news. As Trungpa Rinpoche once said, "The bad news is good news." You're glad to see the news.

Obstacles as teacher: sometimes I also say, poison as medicine. I used the metaphor of a large white canvas, but sometimes I use the metaphor of being in a tight spot. It's the same. Things get very clear when you're cornered. When things are simplified, you always know whether you're on the dot or off the dot.

If someone says, "Be mindful of your breath as it goes out, and let that be the object of your meditation," you notice that and you come back to the outbreath again. You're either with your outbreath or you're not. "Be mindful of drinking tea, be mindful when you put the cup down." You're either right there with the tea cup or you aren't. There's not a lot of room to think about it. That's the notion of precepts, simplifying things so that you can discover.

The ground of any spiritual journey has to be insight, real clear seeing. Another way of expressing this is to talk about the ripening of loving-kindness towards oneself. Loving-kindness has two very important elements. One is a sense of softness, gentleness, not judging. For instance, in meditation technique we're instructed to notice the tone of voice we use when we label the activity "thinking." Sometimes you say it as if it's the enemy. Bang! Like shooting clay pigeons, you want to rid yourself of thought. When this occurs, we're instructed to have a sense of humor about it and

Simplify so you can Discover

say "thinking" with warmth and goodheartedness, so that we aren't engaged in a struggle against our self. It's more a sense of developing a good relationship with our self, based on that softness.

The second and equally important element of loving-kindness (like the second wing of a bird) is precision, accuracy. This friendship with our self isn't based on wishful thinking, or wanting to be better than we are. It's like the relationship with people who are your closest friends. You've been through a lot with them. You know their qualities and you don't have a romantic notion about them. The ground is insight, and it's based on sympathy for oneself based on that insight. In that kind of space, your mind can relax and you don't need this defensiveness of the ego structure. You can relax and let things touch you just as they do, without the sense that they're for you or against you, and without feeling that you either

---

"Fire burns you up, wind blows you into a million pieces, water drowns you, and earth buries you. You're just not there anymore."

---

have to run and hide or develop a new weapon, or find a way to make a nice thing last forever.

In the beginning, the middle, and the end, "obstacle" so-called is a great teacher. It shows you about your own humanity. It shows you how you can perpetuate suffering, and also how you can reduce chaos, your personal chaos and that of the world, through insight. It's like the foundation of a building from which things can begin to develop.

When you start meditation, you begin to see things much more vividly, like that dot on the white canvas. Someone once told me that this was a process of making friends with yourself. Instead, I saw this dreadful stuff and it felt more like becoming my own enemy. That's the point where you can remember that you're not just learning about yourself. In learning about your own jealousy, you're learning about the jealousy of all the human beings who ever lived, are living now or will ever live. You don't have a trite notion of how some philosophical view or an enlightenment weekend will make it all go away. Gradually, you begin to appreciate why other people do what they do.

When my children were young, I first understood why people beat their children. Before that, I had read dreadful things in the newspapers and wondered how anyone could do those things. Suddenly, there I was with my two year old and I understood. Same thing with crimes of passion. I began to understand why people burn down buildings, rape people, why all the painful things happen in the world. It comes from those very same feelings in your heart when you want to do those same things, no matter what they are.

Bite Your Tongue

Your feeling might be quite civilized. Maybe you just want to say what a mean person somebody is. Or maybe they're getting ahead and you want to pass on a little dig that they said, with the intent of slandering them. You know it takes all you can do to bite your tongue. It's that very same kind of little yearning to harm which causes people to do all the things that create chaos in the world. It happens in the individual heart, spreads to families, communities, nations, the whole world, and then to the universe.

Question: So it's the motivation behind the action that counts?

Pema Chödron: If you're willing to work with just not causing harm, you realize that it's certainly possible to break the precepts at the "outer" level, but you can never break them at the level of mind. Your motivation is the main thing. When you begin to understand your own motivation, it's like discovering the whole world. You begin to see why people do what they do, and your compassion isn't just some do-gooder thing like "I'm going to be nice," which inevitably leads to resentment. Your compassion is based on gut level understanding.

When you also understand it isn't necessary to perpetuate that kind of suffering, then your sympathy grows even greater. Your own motivation for practice is to help other people. You may feel that your own understanding is slight, but you realize that you can act and speak out of that understanding. Your motivation is not just based on wanting personal security or getting things comfortable for yourself, or wanting to make life certain and sure. Your motivation becomes wanting to find out the truth and to open up to the whole universe as it is, not as you want it, on your terms.

You could say that the ground is insight, and the path is a sense of beginning to take a genuinely compassionate attitude, some genuine understanding of other people. You realize if you didn't have your obstacles, you would never understand anything. This immediately changes your whole attitude about a sense of "problem" with yourself. It's not at all the same as saying, "Therefore I'm not going to just indulge in my problem," or "I'm going to continue being jealous for the rest of my life."

There's a sense of the richness of the whole process. There's a background of space in which things are always arising and you can really taste it all. Your appetite for life begins to grow. Because of insight and compassion, your discrimination becomes non-discriminating. You'll eat anything, at least once. The metaphor for this is that peacocks eat poison and then have beautiful tails. It's one of the images for a Bodhisattva. You could never eat poison if you didn't first understand it.

That loud sense of "I" or "me" or "I want it" is like a little stronghold. I feel it physically in my body, as if I were a statue carved in stone, when I get so solid about my point of view. When you become sensitive to that solidity, you can understand what renunciation is. For the sake of everyone, you want to let go of holding onto yourself.

As consciousness evolves, obstacles become fuel. They are the very things that blast you into realization. They poke you, prick you, trap you, burn you, freeze you. That's when it's said that you don't need a teacher. Everything in the world becomes your tutor, teaching you all the time about how you close off and how you can open up, how you pretend you're a separate entity and how you realize you aren't.

It is common for everyone committed to the spiritual journey to have an appetite for wanting to live fully. You begin to respect the fact that things don't get simpler, but get more vivid and pointed. The separation between you and the world ceases to be very wide, maybe ceases to exist at all. When something's hot, it is really hot and burns you up. Fire burns you up, wind blows you into a million pieces, water drowns you, and earth buries you. You're just not there anymore. At the same time, fire warms you as it has never warmed you before. The wind in the trees is like hearing the sound of eternity. The earth is your witness, and water is always moving and fluid and endless. You are inseparable from all these things.

As a practitioner on the path and not a realized person, obstacles always still seem like obstacles, but you begin to have a different appetite for them. You're very glad to see that you still have a very small, mean mind, because you don't want it and you're never going to be free of it if you don't see it. It is said that the mark of an enlightened person is a great sense of humor, that without a sense of humor you can never become enlightened. This is encouragement to not just consider all the injustice in the world as a simple matter, and if you got rid of it, it wouldn't be there anymore. There's always going to be more. That's part of the balance. From a historical perspective, some of the worst things and some of the best things have had very unpredictable results.

Everyone has to ask questions forever, but don't be resentful if no one answers your question. No one will ever really answer your question. That's the First Noble Truth. No one can answer it, because you have to discover it for yourself. That's what the Buddha taught. All contemplative people know that. You get inspiration from everything.

I recently made the friendship of an old Native American man whom I respect enormously. In a rather naive way I asked him, "What has been your greatest teacher in life?" He reflected for a while and then said, "Ants. You can learn a lot from ants." ❏

Going Back Into the World

Dr. Joanna Macy

This is our last session. Already our minds are turning to going home, thinking about the families that we are going to reconnect with, and what's up for us tomorrow morning. So it's fitting that in this last session we look directly at our being in the world.

Each of us carries within us an awareness of the suffering of our fellow beings and of what is happening to our planet. Whether we've just started on the Path or have been on it a long time, whether we consider ourselves (as a sister put it so delightfully this morning) a "spiritual mongrel" or have a clear label for our practice and belief system, there is, at some level within us, an awareness that we're not just doing it for ourselves. We sense that the great good fortune that is ours of having encountered the Buddha Dharma, in whatever form we have, has been granted to us for more than our peace of mind, enlightenment, beautification, what have you. There is, perhaps more than at any time when people have come to the Dharma, an awareness that we are doing this practice for the sake of other beings and our world and our planet.

After all these millennia of the human journey on this particular planet, we find ourselves alive in a time when the world can end. This is not a matter of apocalyptic belief but of sober scientific projections and probabilities, given the current behaviors of our species and the forces they have unleashed. Whatever our politics are, we carry that knowledge with us. And what a teacher it is! The very perils of our time can help us to peel back stunning dimensions of the meaning of the Dharma.

Let's bring right up to the front of our minds those knowings in us about what is happening in our world, and what is being prepared, in terms of violence and devastation. We live in a time when, according to the polls, over half the people in this country expect that nuclear war will occur, and that they will not survive it. The psychological implications of that alone are staggering.

We also live in a time when we are destroying our life support system. That is not a potential danger, but a present fact, as is evident in our soil, and in the poisoning of our air, our seas, and in deforestation, desertification, and the extinction of plant and animal species at the rate of three a day. We get these signals not just from television and the press, but in the air we breathe, the water we drink, and what we see around us.

The currents of information that encircle our globe bring us dire warning signals. We are aware of the enormous suffering that is occurring right now with our fellow beings, humans and non-humans. There has probably not been a time in human history when so large a proportion of humanity was without the means for a decent and healthy life.

All this is relevant to our encounter with the Dharma, and we want to take this into account. We don't want our practice to be an escape, but still as we prepare to sit, we sometimes hear an inner voice saying, "Maybe this is a luxury, I should be out and doing." So let's look at what the practice means for our being alive, now.

One of the key teachings of the Buddha is that we have choice. That's what distinguishes humans from all other realms of life: the gods, the devas, the animals. Only humans can change their karma; that is why a human birth is so precious. One of us was talking last night about what it meant to her to think that she had chosen her parents. She felt both empowered and forgiving. Sometimes when we work together on a special project we have the sense of having been brought here by appointments, as if there is some cosmic collusion to our being here alive at this extraordinary time. It's important to get in touch with that sense of privilege and that capacity for choice; it helps us get over any feelings of being victims. It's boring to be a victim.

(At this point Dr. Macy led the participants in a fantasy of choosing their particular reincarnation, a fantasy created by psychiatrist Carol Woolman for helping people deal with the

*psychological fact of living with nuclear weapons. Dr. Macy
closed the meditation by saying, "You are the gift this world has
given itself.)*

Choosing To Be Born A Woman

Last night we were talking about some of the implications of
having chosen to be born women this time around. I believe that
whatever oppression or abuse may have been our lot, as a result of
that, are so many credentials for us. They equip us to heal our world.
It's really important in this planet-time to have some inside track on
what it's like to be oppressed. It's good to look at oppression that
way, because it's easy to get attached to being a victim. As I said
before, that's essentially boring.

It's also important to remember that those who chose to be men

---

"It's really hard to be a man in a dying patriarchy."

---

in this time have their own dukkha (suffering). In our group this
morning one of the men said he had wondered why he came to this
conference. But then he knew; it was so that he could heal his anger
with women. There's a lot of work to do together. I thank him for
having chosen to be born a man. I'm a wife of one and the mother
of two, and I'm telling you, it's really hard to be a man in a dying
patriarchy.

One of the things I really love about the Dharma is the way it
faces straight on what Ruth was reminding us of yesterday, dukkha.
Imagine starting out as a religious teacher and the first thing you say
to people is they are suffering! The Buddha did that! Both feet
smack on the floor: life hurts! That's a good place to begin as we
work in the world, whether we are working with the big issues like
hunger and war or the countless little conflicts, injustices, frustra-
tions in our immediate environment.

It's good to begin with the dukkha because we can really believe it. We believe it because we feel it—and because who would have invented it! There's a lot of pain out there, even among the people who look very successful, competent, affluent, white, middle class, college-educated. They too know pain.

The Saravodya Movement in Sri Lanka similarly begins with that First Noble Truth (that life hurts) when they go into a village to organize. They don't go in without having first been invited. And when they do, they don't come in with blueprints and solutions. Rather they come in and ask people where they hurt. They draw the villagers together into what they call a "family gathering" and invite them to specify their needs. In the process, the villagers experience their own expertise: they *are* experts on what is not working for them.

"Life hurts! That's a good place to begin as we work in the world."

If there's one thing that's similar between our life in the post-industrial West and village life in Southeast Asia, it's a feeling of powerlessness. You begin overcoming that right away by noting your own expertise about what's wrong. Who's the expert on your needs? *You* are!

So we can begin at the same place in our culture. I have been doing that with the despair and empowerment work here and in other countries. This work helps people get in touch with their own painful responses to what is happening to our planet. Responses to being alive in a world that can include grief, the sorrow that arises when you look at the face of your child, or when you want to have a child. They include fear—dread of what's in store for us and what we're creating. They include anger, a stifled rage that we have let it come to this, and they include disbelief and guilt.

Those responses are natural, they are normal and even wholesome, but our culture as a whole is stuck in a place of not wanting to experience them. That's what is called "psychic numbing." Our culture will do almost anything not to experience the grief, anger, fear, and sorrow that is right there below the surface of business-as-usual. The buying sprees and hedonism, the rise in suicide rates and drug abuse, the blaming, cultism, fundamentalism, name-calling, and hate-filled diatribes against the victims of your choice— blacks, Jews, homosexuals, women, you name it—all of that stems from not wanting to look at the hurt that's inside, the dukkha.

Intrinsic to that denial is a semiconscious fear that we might break or shatter if we allow ourselves to experience that pain. So it's very important for us to have an experience of the Buddha Dharma so that we don't break when we experience suffering. With Dharma practice we need not be afraid of experiencing sorrow and fear, we need not run from them, we're not fragile, skin-encapsulated egos.

The Great Compassion

Thich Nhat Hanh says that what we most need to do right now is hear within ourselves the sounds of the earth crying. That pain is product and proof of our interrelatedness with all beings. Dukkha can open us right into the heart of reality where all beings coexist, inter-exist like jewels in the net of Indra.

What you discover when you open to the suffering of our time is that you are encountering your own compassion. Only it isn't your own, it's the great compassion, the Mahakaruna. This is important to remember: you wouldn't be feeling it if we were not intricately connected, and if you were not, thanks to these connections, compassionate. It's like signs of life from that body which is your larger body.

The pain you feel for those in the hunger camps, the refugee camps, the prison camps, the war rooms, the missile silos, the barracks, the nursing homes, the school rooms, or even the face in the mirror, it is like the sensation in a phantom limb. It is said that when you have a leg amputated, you still feel twinges and that is called a "phantom limb." What I'm talking about is phantom limb in reverse. We have been raised thinking that our body ended here, with this bag of skin, or with our possessions or our education or house. Now we begin to realize that our body is the world. Our pain tells us that.

As you experience grief with the grief of others, so can you know joy with the joy of others. The Buddhist name for this is "mudita." As we open to our interexistence as fellow beings, we open not only to their suffering, but also to their resources, their gifts, and to the power going through them. This is really important for Westerners to get.

In the Western religious traditions we honor compassion, but we're not very good at the flip side, mudita. That's one of the first things that delighted me in Buddhism. Mudita, by the way, is a

---

"Our culture will do almost anything not to experience grief, anger, fear, and sorrow ..."

---

great antidote to envy. It allows you to look at your fellow beings and open to their power and beauty and resources—gifts and resources you can draw from like money in the bank.

The courage of a Mohandas K. Gandhi or a Martin Luther King or a Dorothy Day didn't die with them. We live in a holographic universe, or as imaged by Buddhists, the jeweled net of Indra. No acts are lost. We can train ourselves to draw on the resources that are already there. We didn't come into this universe alone, we have all these brothers and sisters and we can take their gumption, ingenuity, faithfulness, endurance and let it flow into and through us. Whew, what a relief! We don't need to dredge up from ourselves all the courage and love that is needed. The very deprivation and exhaustion that we may feel can be the opportunity to open to our interexistence with others.

It's like grace. In the Christian tradition, grace comes largely

from God. The Buddhists show us that each of us is the occasion
of grace, a resource.

Turning the Wheel

I want to talk a moment about turning. In the Buddhist tradition,
we talk about the turning of the wheel of Dharma. When the old
Buddhist teachings came in new form in Mahayana Buddhism, it
was called the second turning of the wheel. This balancing of
Buddhism in the late twentieth century (not just in America but for
Buddhists around the world) is another turning of the wheel.

For a wheel to turn, it must be empty in the middle.

The Dharma, in that regard, offers a fresh source of imagery of
the feminine. One image in particular has been very powerful for
me: Prajnaparamita, the Perfection of Wisdom, the mother of all
the Buddhas. She first emerges over two thousand years ago in the
earliest of Mahayana texts. These texts set forth the Bodhisattva
path, that is, the path of one who, at the gates of Nirvana, turns and
comes back again, vowing to keep returning to this side of reality
until all beings are enlightened—for the Bodhisattva knows he or
she is not separate from all beings. I like Prajnaparamita because
she doesn't fit into the kind of masculine-feminine imagery you get
in most other cultures, which posits a sky=father and earth=mother,
setting up opposition between feeling and intellect, between mind
and matter.

We have been raised in a culture where female is to male as
nature is to cultures, as earth is to sky, etc. I'm really bored with it!
One of the gifts that Buddhist women can bring to the women's
movement is to tell them to get off it about equating the feminine
with emotionality and the masculine with reason. The Perfection
of Wisdom is *wisdom*, and she's the mother of the Buddhas. She's
not sky or earth, she's symbolized by space. A term that is used for
her is "deep space." She is a deep space in which, as the old texts
say, the Bodhisattva flies like a bird, where there is nothing to hang
onto, no crutches or easy answers, no quick or guaranteed solution.

Dr. Joanna Macy

It is the space you dis-
cover when you let your-
self stop hanging onto
your self-images and neu-
roses, when you stop tak-
ing yourself so seriously,
when you stop clutching
at the self whether it's to
improve or punish it, to
mortify or sacrifice it. I
was fascinated to discover
a treatise on mathematics
explaining the origin of
"zero." Zero was a revo-
lutionary development, a
quantum leap in human
understanding. Before

that, no concept or sign existed to mark and hold the empty decimal
place, sorely limiting the capacity to compute. It originated in
India, I learned, brought to Europe by Moslem traders who put it
into the Arabic numeral system. In ancient India, zero was known
by name before a symbol for it developed. There were several
names: *sunya* (empty), *purna* (full), *nada* (navel), *akasa* (space),
and *ka*. At this point in my reading I almost shouted in astonishment
and glee because these very terms were, I recognized, how the early
Mahayana texts characterized Prajnaparamita; they were her at-
tributes! The mother of the Buddha was also the mother of zero,
revolutionizing mathematics.

Furthermore, *ka*, the last term mentioned, means the hole in the
hub of the wheel through which the axle passes. It must be empty
and round like an O, like a vagina, if the wheel is to turn. Only by
letting go into the apparent emptiness beyond ego can the wheel of
the Dharma turn again in one time. It is an emptiness that is a
fullness *(purna)* too, because in it we awaken to our interrelatedness with all beings, or as Thich Nhat Hanh calls it, our "interbeing."

85

That is what the Buddha woke up to under the bodhi tree, the dependent co-arising of all phenomena, and that vividly intricate interplay is what later Mahayanists imaged in the jeweled net of Indra.

I suggest to you who have chosen to be women in this incarnation, and have been fortunate enough to encounter the Dharma, that we have a particularly rewarding mission. We can bring to our time—to our practice and our world—this heightened sense of interrelatedness. By our conditioning as well as our biology, we tune to relationships, can intuitively grasp the relational nature of the universe, the net of Indra.

As we go out into the world, we can let every encounter, every relationship become an occasion for flying within the deep space of the Perfection of Wisdom. Each event can become the occasion for experiencing the power of interdependence and the practicality of peace.

"For a wheel to turn, it must be empty in the middle."

You may remember that in the early scriptures the Buddha was asked, "Do we need to perform sacrifices to get to the realm of the Brahma?" (This was the chief Vedic god.) The Buddha said, "You can be there already by practicing *metta* (loving kindness), *karuna* (compassion), *mudita* (joy in the joy of others), and *uppeka* (equanimity)." In the Sarvodaya movement, these qualities are conveyed in ways that help people take charge of their lives and then move right out to work together in organizing for community development. That's what I mean when I speak of this being an historic time for Buddhism.

Some of you may be familiar with liberation theology in the Christian tradition, widespread in South and Central America. It emphasizes the revolutionary teachings of Jesus and uses them to empower people to work for liberation and social change. This is an epic development, and I can see the same thing happening in Buddhism. The social teachings of the Buddha, which can be seen as economically and politically revolutionary, were institutionalized into static hierarchies. Now the potency of his teachings for social change is being brought to the fore. I should put in a plug here for the Buddhist Peace Fellowship, a force for "engaged Buddhism," and I hope you will get to know the work of Thich Nhat Hanh.

Your lives are woven inextricably in the jeweled net of Indra, as interwoven as neurons in the mind of a great being. You cannot fall out of that web. No stupidity, cowardice, or failure can ever separate you from that living net, because that is what you are. Rest in that knowing, come home to it. In that is the Great Peace. Out of that you can risk everything, knowing that each encounter can be a coming home again to that Great Peace. Indeed, it is so. ❏

How To Balance A White Cloud

Gesshin Prabhasa Dharma, Roshi

Dear friends, I am really happy to be here and continue where we left off last year, at the conference of Women in American Buddhism, looking at the situation of Buddhism in the U.S. and the emergence of a new tradition. "The Balancing of American Buddhism" is a challenging title since it implies some kind of need to balance. Whether the need to change arises from frustration in personal teacher-disciple relationships, or issues forth from a more fundamental dissatisfaction with the current ethnological division of American Buddhists, remains to be investigated.

Clearly there is a need to clarify our direction. When we began to practice Zen and study Dharma some twenty years ago, we first needed to immerse ourselves completely in the forms that Asian Buddhist traditions brought to us. Now, some twenty years later, we are emerging, realizing the need to integrate the Buddhist Way of Life into our own social structure and culture. This presents a great opportunity for a new and fresh interpretation of Buddhism in a modern world.

But how do we balance, and, more importantly, what needs to be balanced? Wanting to balance presupposes that one knows the norm, knows what is "real." To know what is real means to be aware of the great fluidity of the changing patterns of events, like clouds in the sky constantly changing their shapes. Clearly we cannot change the patterns of the clouds. But what can be changed is our perception mechanism. Change means to leave the fixated position of personal perspective and acquire the wisdom of cosmic consciousness. In the realm of cosmic consciousness there is no division between self and other. In direct identification we can only say "not two." All is lucid and self-illuminating.

Very often the general non-Buddhist public looks at Buddhists who meditate as being "non-active," not properly engaged in the world. This view is based on the notion that to benefit the human world one must do something in an active and material way. True compassion, however, is ultimately much more profoundly expressed in *how* we are rather than in actions coming from dualistic awareness. Inactivity and activity are inseparable from each other.

As we sit in meditation, we learn that what we usually call the activity of the world is nothing other than our own consciousness set in motion. When consciousness is at rest, there is peace. When individual self is not interfering, we see true Dharma activity, and for the first time we see things as they are. This seeing, such as it is, is the balance we have searched for. It is the end of desire, and peace of mind ensues. When self is identified with the alternating cosmic cycles of activity/inactivity, we have perfect balance. After working we need to rest. After resting we can work again.

"We are answerable for all our actions in spite of ignorance and erroneous beliefs."

No living being can ever be separate from this perfect activity; every living thing is merely a manifestation of this cosmic activity. In the opening passage of the Diamond Sutra we find a description of the activities of the Lord Buddha:

> *Near dawn, the Lord clothed himself, took up his bowl and entered the great city of Sravasti to collect food offered as alms. Having returned and eaten, the Lord put away his bowl and cloak, bathed his feet and sat with legs crossed and body upright upon the seat arranged for him, mindfully fixing attention in front of himself .... At that moment the Venerable Subhuti arose from his seat and showing real respect for the Buddha, said, It is wonderful, most wonderful, O Lord, how much the Tathagata, the Fully Enlightened One, has helped the Bodhisattvas protecting and instructing them.*

We usually read over this passage quickly to get to the meaning of the Sutra. Yet here in this opening paragraph we have the complete instruction of a Fully Enlightened One living in the world of human beings, in every activity fulfilling the cosmic Law. The fullness of the cosmic Law, the purity of its miraculous function, lies at the root of every activity. To live in Pure Knowledge of the unbounded potential and its great function is to be properly engaged in the world.

This cosmic Law is beyond all the ethnic differentiations of the various traditions and yet it finds its mode of expression just exactly in those various traditions. Becoming enlightened, realizing the cosmic Law as the ultimate reality, leads us to freedom from material illusions and thus to a new understanding of the appropriateness of the material as such. It belongs to the foolishness of the ignorant mind to dismiss what cannot be perceived as matter as "unreal."

But we are answerable for all our actions in spite of ignorance and erroneous beliefs. And if we do not realize this cosmic Law to be our own mind essence, we will continue to be dissatisfied and suffer endless rebirths until we learn and accept the true nature of things. From the point of view of this absolute truth, the cosmic Law and its great function are never out of order. A Zen Master was asked, "What eyes will you use to teach the people of this world?" and he responded, "The sun and the moon have never been out of order."

You Are The White Cloud Itself

The enlightened person is the Total Person, one who flows effortlessly with the Dharma. The word "person" is derived from the Latin "per"—through—and "sonair"—to sound. The Total Person, then, is one through whom ultimate reality, such as it is, is "sounding." If you are lying in the grass looking at a white cloud drifting through the sky, you are the white cloud itself. At that moment, if there is no thought of cloud or self, you are in perfect balance. It is only thought that sets us apart from the enlightened state of mind. The notion of imperfection arises from imbalance in individual consciousness, from being out of sync with the greater activity of the cosmos. In studying the activity of the universe, we find that all superficially differentiated events are unified on the level of the underlying principle of coherence and mutual penetration.

Through a maze of infinite possibilities and multiplicities, the activity of the Dharma always takes the course of the least action. It organizes spontaneously by using the least amount of activity. Thus it is seen as absolutely serene, showing no signs of becoming and yet always going along with the arising and dissolution of the momentary phenomenal events, without being disturbed by them. "Calm, yet freely moving, unknowing in itself, unified and non-

---

"Buddhism in America will reflect our advancements in science, technology and social structure."

---

discriminating, it is at the same time functioning in every possible way, and is able to discern everything."[1]

If there is only the will to change and to do good, and fundamental insight into the true nature of things is lacking, we will merely repeat the same mistakes, continuing activity which is based upon erroneous thinking. The sense of balance occurs when the right view of the cosmic Law and its function is gained by the individual. Reaching deeper into oneself means reaching increased order, hence the Zen Master's proclamation: "The sun and the moon have never been out of order." The universe itself in its twofold mode of appearance and disappearance, as form and non-form, is the

---

[1]Ven. Gesshin Prabhasa Dharma, Roshi, *Going Home* (Los Angeles, International Zen Institute of America), page 5.

example of perfect coherence and harmony of all fields of activity effortlessly moving from one level of systems to another, spontaneously transforming, always taking the course of least effort, of the least energy expense.

In Buddhism, balancing means that the individual comes into the knowledge of the full potential of the Dharma in his/her own consciousness and enters into the process of self-regulation of the individual.

The new field, then, where a new tradition can grow is the field of our own consciousness. And new form will emerge naturally from being firmly grounded in this spiritual realization of the unified field of cosmic consciousness. What American Buddhists wear and eat and how they are going to carry out compassionate social activities will naturally evolve from this integration of individual, personal views into the fundamental field of cosmic order. Neither Japanese nor Tibetan nor any other form of Buddhism will be the Buddhism of Americans. Buddhism in America will necessarily reflect our advancements in science, technology, and social structure. This is not only an opportunity for a new beginning, but also the only possibility. Last but not least, it is our responsibility toward the world of all living beings to develop new systems based on "real activity."

The New Age Being

This new tradition of the Total Person, the transcendent personality, will find its expression in a new way of relating to what was hitherto seen as "self" and "other" and "the world." The Total Person is the new-age being, totally awake and aware, at peace with him/herself and interacting in a loving and caring way with all forms of life as well as with all non-forms. The Total Person expresses respect for all things, but relies only on Dharma, realizing that by far the greater power and stability are not to be found in the world of objects and ideas, but in their underlying principle of emptiness. Emptiness or non-form is the ultimate mode of form—

and ultimate form is liberation.

Ordinary human existence is frustrating and unsatisfactory until we gain insight into the nature of Real Life. The full discovery of this Potential of human consciousness has within it the seeds for growth and a power for development never yet realized on this earth. It has the power to blaze the trail for the equality of beings of all races, cultures, and nations; and for the opportunity to live in harmony and peace with each other on this planet earth, our temporary home. In the words of Dr. Albert Einstein:

> *The religion of the future will be a cosmic religion. It should transcend a personal God and avoid dogmas and theology. Covering both the natural and the spiritual, it should be based on a religious sense of arising from the experience of all things natural and spiritual as a meaningful unity. Buddhism answers this description .... If there is any religion that would cope with modern scientific needs it would be Buddhism.*

I cannot think of a better place for this to come to fruition than in the socio-political structure of North America.

May all beings attain enlightenment and grow as happy as they can be. ❑

A Tea Ceremony

Gesshin Prabhasa Dharma, Roshi

Another aspect of realizing is to have moments of silence in our lives. This afternoon we will practice this in the tea ceremony. The Japanese have created a way in which leaders and servants, masters and assistants, and even children from a certain age on up sit together and everyone is regarded as equal.

This sense of equality becomes apparent even in the structure of the tea rooms. A tea room in Japan does not have a standard-sized doorway. It has a tiny two foot opening in the wall, through which you practically have to crawl into the tea room. Whether you are the president or the president's assistant, you have to crawl through this door. Even though at the end of the tea we wear different clothes and show other signs of difference, in the tea ceremony we are all regarded as the same.

It is the same with the tea master, who takes responsibility to guide us through the event. Tea is for tea; it's not just a culturally beautiful thing to do. I'm presenting it because I would like to suggest that all political meetings, all summit conferences, should start this way with people going into the room through a small door, sitting in a circle around a conference table, and having a cup of tea together followed by a few moments of silence and mindful awareness.

What distinguishes us from animals is that while animals are one with the Dharma, they don't know it. They cannot enjoy it. They live in fear and anxiety. We human beings, who have the capacity for deep meditation and for coming back from that disappearing act into a consciousness in which we can reflect on that, can come into the full enjoyment of living the Dharma here and now as it is. This is how we must begin to make peace in the world, not thinking that we have to do something "out there" to change it. What we

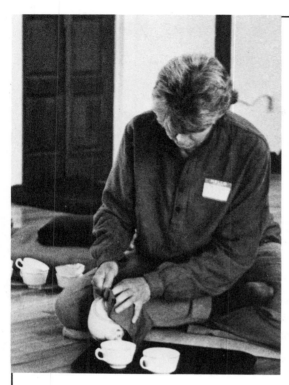

In my always
planning ahead
I almost missed
the steam
coming from
my cup of tea

Two hands
One teacup
Never empty
Never full

Hot tea,
blue rug
There is
nothing
so difficult
about this
practice

are saying when we do that is that it is the others *who have no peace and that* they *need to be taught.*

What is nice about the tea ceremony and the way we're going to do it is that you are both "host" and "guest." At the moment you receive the tea from one side, you are the guest. When you put your cup down and pass the tray to your neighbor, you are the host. In the world you should realize constantly that you are the "all." When Jesus realized the truth, he said, "I am the all." Buddha said, "The Dharma and I are one. When you want to see the real me, look at the Dharma. When you want to see the Dharma, look at me."

When we do this tea ceremony, we should first collect ourselves, like the Buddha did. Take your seat mindfully, arrange your clothes around you. When you are seated, sit a few moments in silence. Then we will drink tea together with the whole universe.

I want you to contribute something to the ceremony in the form of a word, a poem, or music. I would like you not to be tense about having something already created, but trust your intuition. Enjoy the tea, and then let come up just exactly what comes.

Thank you all for your patience. ❏

Panel Discussion

Saturday, September 14, 1985

Question: I feel a little disappointed in the content of the conference so far. I've come to the last two and it's been important to me in exploring the new edges of Buddhism in America. My interpretation of this conference is that it's a continuation of the last two years of talking about the new edge in Buddhism and feminism. Why was feminism not mentioned today? Is it tomorrow's agenda?

Ruth Denison: I didn't go into it because I referred to the bottom line, the teachings of the Buddha, how he gave pure ground rules and how we can follow them and perhaps manifest them more easily and with a little haste. If we attend to the teachings, feminism is not a separate issue any more. At the same time, going to the source is not overlooking or ruling out the details. As a teacher I represent the Women's Sangha in Berkeley and there too, we always go to the basic teachings and relate them to daily problems which may arise. If you have a special issue or question within feminism, I can go into that. In general, if we are well-equipped and see balance, insight, and wisdom growing in ourselves, we will be getting a lot of answers from our own insides and our own security.

Prabhasa Dharma: I agree with Ruth. I think if we want to deal with anything and learn from it, we must be very specific and concrete. Feminism to me is an abstract word. I'm quite sure there may be a number of people here in the room who share the same understanding of what it means, but I'm not sure what all of us understand. We'd first have to clarify what we mean by that word, feminism. Could you give us a specific example?

Question: I felt that some of the issues you raised in the last conference seemed very vital to me. For example, some of the things you spoke about specific to an American type of Buddhism, how we as Americans receive this practice in our own special way, what it means for our work in the world—the work we do for money, and as parents, and so forth. Many more householders, laypeople, in the country are Buddhist now and that means special kinds of problems and special kinds of openings. Also, Dr. Macy talked about Buddhist Peace Fellowship and other such organizations, other applied aspects of Buddhism, which means new openings. So, how much should we sit on our cushions, how much should we go out into the world? How do we decide that for ourselves individually, and how as Americans?

Prabhasa Dharma: Okay. Well, one great thing that the Buddha has done was that he was a social reformer, too. He made women equal to men in his sangha. So I don't want to undo that, to separate male and female. Everything that I said today applies to both men and women. But in the relative world, if you look at our human bodies, there are male and female bodies with different energies, and we may have different ways of expressing this basic teaching in the world. You may have a particular problem which I also had when I started out on the path, but because I followed the Buddha's path (that already complete system he developed that can be approached in many different ways—softer or harder, higher or lower levels), I learned how to solve these problems.

Basically, that is how Zen works in the world. It doesn't deal with issues *per se*, but with the individual, to make you free whether you're a man or woman, so you can be the master of yourself and handle these problems, give your own answers to your questions. Culturally you have a situation here that's different from the Orient. For example, here at Providence Zen Center there is a couple who could have a husband and wife abbotship and take turns leading the temple, presuming they have equal training. Basically, we will never solve problems by looking and going at them with the old tools we have used in the past. So, I'm willing to listen to very specific problems, but I cannot help you on the level of feminism, because I didn't study or work in that. I was practicing Zen at that time.

Question: Well, what about approaching this from another direction? Going into almost any training center in this country where there's a man teacher in charge, it's pretty easy to see a certain amount of favoritism for a man, an approach to power that is not equilateral or sharing or a consensus approach. It's very hierarchical.

Prabhasa Dharma: I'm sure you have seen many such cases, but still we cannot generalize, because there are also cases where

---

As American women opening to the Dharma, we're participating in something beyond our own little scenarios. I believe we're reclaiming the equality of the sexes in the Buddhadharma.

---

women have become leaders of centers. In my own case, I had to follow my own very strongly arising intuition and wisdom. Then maybe there has to be a thing as cutting the umbilical cord. Go away from the teacher when you're ready and be on your own. I think a lot of people are afraid of that. Maybe there isn't enough experience and trust of oneself to do that, to step right out and say, "I'm ready to listen to the wisdom as it arises in me."

We could make a mistake if we further cultivate the discriminating consciousness by continually making issues out of "me" and "them." That's what I'm trying to avoid. Based upon reality, there have to be male leaders and female leaders, men and women teachers. They're evolving, they're here. Zen practice is to live by what you have learned. I don't often talk about it because I feel by just being what I am, that's an indication of how I've dealt with it.

It's possible. You have to have will-power and trust and energy, which you get from meditation. You can do anything in this world. You can become President of the United States.

Question: I'd like to give the analogy of the racial situation. There's no doubt that specific blacks were absolutely mistreated by Americans and other white countries a hundred years ago. But we blame them for being stupid, when in fact it was illegal a hundred years ago for a black person to get an education. The situation in most countries now is that women do have that power and they don't seem very anxious to continue that power.

Prabhasa Dharma: You must first deal with yourself, your own problem, and get clear about that. Then you'll be able to help others, but not before that. That is what I did. For something like eighteen years I practiced very hard. I didn't go out much to teach or try to do something about the world. We are taught by the Buddha first to understand the nature of self and the world, and to realize they are not two different things. When that has occurred, then we are more useful to the world. You can help just by being present.

We have made overly sophisticated the discriminating consciousness. We try to do everything with that consciousness, politically, socially, whatever. It is quite correct that we have compassion for others, but it's not true compassion if it's based on discrimination, even the discrimination of "me" and "other." Compassion is important, but it's dangerous to act too soon.

Joanna Macy: I'd like to add an historical note. I see Buddhism as a tradition having suffered under several thousand years of patriarchy. As a movement of Buddhism, in Vipassana there is a return, a balancing within the Buddhadharma to seeing more clearly the male-dominated, hierarchic patterns that have arisen in the last two millennia. You can trace this specifically in historical developments.

This is happening in other cultures too. I've been working with the Sarvodaya movement, a Buddhist-inspired community development program in South Asia, very big in about 5000 villages. Women are coming to the fore in this movement. There is also a conscious return, which scholars are participating in, to reclaim the role that women had in early pre-Theravadan Buddhism. It's a little harder than in Christianity, because there are misogynist passages written right into the sutras, but you can show by language and text analysis that these were later additions.

I want to say that as American women opening to the Dharma, we're participating in something beyond our own little scenarios. I believe we are finding ourselves reclaiming the equality of the sexes in the Buddhadharma. We're participating in a balancing of Buddhism that has great historic significance, and I think we can

---

"Buddhism as we live it is not a dead structure or a dogma."

---

take a sense of amplitude in that. We're not just fighting our own little battles here, but we're righting or balancing history. It feels good! *(laughter)*

Pema Chödron: If you look at the history of mankind, there's always been this natural evolution of balancing. Things get out of balance, people feel it, then things get balanced again. It keeps going back and forth, in longer or shorter periods of time. It's not just at the personal level that so many women feel things are out of balance. Things are out of balance! *(laughter)* It's not just some personal little weight that you are carrying around because someone is out to get you. It's an historical time when actually it's very positive.

Things are shifting so that the balance is going towards more feminine energy. My feeling is that it isn't a matter of letting feminine energy surge up and masculine energy go down, but that in every individual the balance of masculine and feminine energy needs to be found. Men feel as well as women that things are out of balance. For the last ten years people have been speaking out about it. It's a natural organic thing like the seasons. I have a favorite quote from Tai Situ Rinpoche who was asked, "Why are there no women rinpoches?" And he said, "Well, that's history. Now it's up to you." *(laughter)*

Prabhasa Dharma: Actually, things are not out of balance. *(laughter)* It depends on from what level we look at it. We think things are out of balance because things are shifting now. But in reality, they're not out of balance. Until now, we have had pretty much a male-created world, for instance, the whole world of technology. I don't know if women would have been thinking about the world in the same way, producing in the same way. This is not to say we're not capable of it, but that maybe we would have dealt with things a little differently.

You all know *Star Wars* and *E.T.* Both are films about outer space, fantasy about other creatures. *Star Wars* is warfare in outer space with weapons and sophisticated machinery and uniforms, about a toy world that men imagine. *E.T.* was written by a woman, *Star Wars* by a man. *E.T.* deals with an individual from another planet and the feelings and relationships between two children and this creature. It's a totally different approach to the science fiction of outer space.

The Dharma has these two aspects. Male, active, manifesting, matter—these are the labels we have put on this forward creating movement. The same movement when it goes back, within, home, one could label as spiritual or dissolving matter. It is usually associated with the feminine and even called negative or death. So the universe is always in balance. When it has manifested so much matter, it has to go back and provide the balance, that is a more feminine energy in the forefront. It shouldn't mean feminism. It should mean that we're all participating in it.

Ruth Denison (right) and interested students.

We have to let go of this over-producing, matter kind of hardware world. In the world of computers, you have to have hardware and software. *(laughter)* So it's not out of balance, but our viewing of it that's out of balance. This is what the Buddha gave us the right and power to do. He said, "The Dharma is in you just as it is in me." So you begin to act and live in it.

●

Question: One of the issues that's most painful to talk about, for women who go through training, is having had male teachers. Although the Buddhist teachings are fair and equal, all teachers do not manifest this teaching in a fair way. All teachers do not challenge the biases within and the male ego they carry with them, because they are not challenged by their teachers to do so. I and maybe other women too have had to leave teachers because of direct and indirect abuse.

Panel Discussion

Pema Chödron: So what did you do?

Question: I left.

Pema Chödron: And then? You're still alive.

Question: And I'm continuing to practice. But there are people who are teaching, who taught me, who practiced for twenty years and still ripped me off.

Prabhasa Dharma: What you were saying about your personal story, I deeply feel with you because I went through that myself. I'm here as an example of what one can do with that. Maybe you can do something different with it. I don't think we can make rules about this to solve the problem. That is why we always go so deep and say that basically, we must become whole and healed. Then we find our role and will evolve as a teacher, no matter what we do, even if we become bakers or something, we will be a teacher. We will find a way to manifest what we most want to be. This is what I believe in.

Question: Ideally all things are in balance. But that person is still causing pain to other people. I can heal and go to practice, but what happens to the others?

Pema Chödron: I think it's a question of how you relate to injustice in the world, any injustice, even if it's someone hurting your cat. How do you relate to things not being right? It brings up self-doubt. Otherwise, why wouldn't you just blast out in a nonaggressive way? *(laughter)* If you have confidence.

Question: This is your Buddhist teacher. You've taken vows with this person. This person is experienced and has more sitting wisdom, intuition coming forth than you. And this person does something to you. Certainly you grow a lot, but I don't think you ever get to be sure.

Pema Chödron: When you stand in the hallway outside this room, you can see the calligraphy that says, Bodhidharma sat for nine years and in spite, he killed the Buddha. Then you say, that's what it means.

Question: The problem of isolation is one I've felt most acutely. I've come to a conference like this specifically to hear things brought up because I spend a lot of my time alone. I'm a single mother with two small children. It's actually a battle to make that time to sit every day. Last year Jan Chozen spoke with such beautiful humor about being in the bathroom and having a kid pounding on the door. It's enough to run into a situation of daily life, never mind injustice, when you have no community around

---

"Bad teacher, good teacher, that's a teacher."

---

you to say, "Yes, we felt this too and what you've gone through is very troubling." I wonder why we're afraid to say the name of a person who's causing trouble. Somehow we need to have a network.

●

Prabhasa Dharma: There are already a lot of women teachers in this country. If you have problems with men teachers, just go to the women teachers.

Question: And let them continue using people? Just ignore them and go away?

Prabhasa Dharma: One thing I've learned in this country is that businesses go out of business when you don't buy their product. *(laughter and applause)* But we have to be very, very careful. The Buddha said, hatred is not appeased by hatred. If we find something wrong and take the same measures and attitudes and weapons to strike back, then we're no better. We're in the same club.

Question: Which guru or rinpoche or whatever is doing this? We'll put up a list here. I think that would be great. If people have had these experiences, I think it should be out immediately. We all love truth, don't we? That's why we're here. Seriously, let's look the Buddha right in the face. I'm not saying you shouldn't have compassion, but does that mean you have compassion for the cat who eats the mouse, and for the mouse who dies, so you stand by and watch? "Ah, nature! Dukkha!" When does one take political action, and when does one sit and meditate?

Ruth Denison: On such issues, one can use one's intelligence and the quality of observing closely, which has kind of an objective attitude. First you get a bit of distance. Then you will be able to see in that space what possibility there is for you to directly touch that problem. That is my way of dealing with problems. I have a lot of criticism about injustice, but I don't allow myself to be contaminated by any reaction to it.

Some kind of objectivity is necessary because if I allow myself to be too involved with criticism, I am too much in the process and have no energy left to see my opportunity for helping. As Prabhasa already said, because of that momentary impact, it's impossible for you to help or do anything without accumulating some other karma or contaminating your heart with anger. We need an immediate relaxing and pacifying. I fall back to the First Noble Truth. Why do you think the Buddha spoke as a result of his enlightenment? To give a truth, the truth of suffering and imperfection and what we have to go through.

If you can, just keep the energies alive and awake and train a bit more for what is necessary, until you are more capable. Most of why we are not able to get into this, but stand back and talk about injustice, is we're not capable or we doubt ourselves. As Pema said, strike! Provided you have immaculately investigated your possible effectiveness so that you can now not just grossly enter that event,

but sensitively. It doesn't need to be big compassion, but just a little. Be modest, take the crumbs and don't wait for the whole loaf, or until it is your enlightenment. We will never make it. Meanwhile, we will be destroyed. Use the moment to moment opportunity with the possibilities you have.

I can give you many little examples where I took the crumbs and brought about changes in attitude about wrong-doing in my neighbors and students. I am very involved in environmental help. Two nights a week, at least, I have this suitcase full of requests for help from environmental societies. I cannot give to every one. And if I cannot, I will sit down and write, "I appreciate your efforts in diminishing the suffering of our friends the animals, or for the protection of the wilderness," and so on. At least I can give encouragement. That is a little crumb that I can do.

We have to work with what's here, and to incessantly, untiringly work and sleep only three to four hours. Work hard. Only this way will we get over the evil here. Train your mind with recollection. See where you can be practical. Never function on generalities and the hypothetical. That doesn't mean you can't look at issues and deal with them on an intellectual level—don't let this aspect slip. Too much involvement will take away energies from looking at things the way they really are. Then you might have had a chance but you didn't see it. The world is always full of opportunity for us to help.

Think of that First Noble Truth. It is deep. The world is full of suffering and was 2500 years ago. It is more staggering now. Dukkha is fat! See the place where you can help, carrying this dukkha with your little love and touching. Help the mother or goddess of the earth with your crumb, your little love. I think you can produce a lot.

Question: I wanted to say something without taking anything away from what people have said about being abused by a teacher. It's been an opportunity for growth for me, to examine bad experiences with Dharma teachers and other people to whom I've given authority. What was it in me that chose someone and gave power to someone who would abuse me in some way? What was it in my and that other person's conditioning that put us together in a place where we would use each other in that way?

It's true that if someone is a teacher, you have a right to expect them to be more responsible than you, to know more than you. Nevertheless, I have observed in myself a willingness to absolve myself of responsibilities, a naive willingness to believe that this person is something bigger than human. I've had to re-examine what is a master and what do I want from a master. Although one has a right to expect (to put it mildly) good behavior from a master, in places where there was someone to whom I have given power, I have given up responsibility for what happens in that relationship.

It is give and take with a teacher and no matter how badly I've

---

"After all these millenia of the human journey on this planet, we find ourselves alive in a time when the world can end."

---

been hurt, every time I've had a bad experience, I've learned. That's part of what happens with growing up and with any relationship. You get hurt and then you learn and come to terms with the ways in which you were responsible for a part of what happened. It doesn't just happen with Dharma teachers or just with women. It happens to men too. I know a lot of men who have been deeply hurt in relationships with Dharma teachers.

This kind of abuse happens when there is someone to whom a lot of power is given and someone who doesn't take responsibility. Male-female relationships, relationships with Dharma teachers, are ripe for that because of our long-term conditioning in which men have more power and are taught to use it, and women are taught to give in to it. Nonetheless, that person is a victim of the same conditioning and on some level is being hurt by what they're doing.

Bad teacher, good teacher, that's a teacher. You have learned and there's some level on which you can be grateful for what has happened, when the pain goes away.

There is teaching in everything. Even when there's no abuse involved within the Dharma, the teaching process is frequently painful on some emotional level.

Joanna Macy: You have raised a point which is critically important, the connection between being victimized and understanding what power is. In this time in which we're living, particularly those of us who have such good karma as to have been exposed to the Dharma are challenged to help people within and without the Buddha-sangha redefine what power is. The teachers who are abusing are often people who have been isolated and put into a position of power. It takes two to tango.

I mentioned the Sarvodaya movement. I did assertiveness training there, put in Buddhist terms. We didn't call it assertiveness training (this was just for Sri Lankan and Singalese Buddhist women), we called it the Middle Path. *(laughter and applause)* That's the middle path between belligerence and submission. We had such a good time. *(laughter)* And it came right down to seeing how central is our understanding of power. The Sarvodaya movement talks about the goal of building people's power. But goodness, we don't have to buy into hierarchic understandings of what power is, because we've got the central teaching of the Lord Buddha himself, of dependent co-arising, that power is essentially relational and reciprocal.

So this is a plea for all of us now to rethink and re-image power so that we don't fall into the hierarchic games. The Dharma has clearer directions and foundations than any other system of thought that I know about. That's why women have such a strong role to play now for all Buddhists, male or female. It's because (to use Carol Gilligan's term) we are socialized to be very sensitive to relationship.

Question: Teachers are human. We see teachers behaving in certain ways out of their human need, and they're a little mad at us because they think we have too high expectation. I'm glad to hear you say that new students and new teachers can alter that structure. How do you view the role of teachers? Sometimes I think they do want it all ways, like yuppies, they want to be wonderful mothers and have great sex relationships and be successful in their jobs. *(laughter)* How deeply do you feel you owe your students exemplary behavior?

Pema Chödron: I have had the good fortune to have a teacher who is famous for his bad behavior. *(laughter)* Also he likes hierarchy a lot. We have an extremely hierarchic organization. It's interesting what that does to your mind when you're brought up in that tradition. The first thing it teaches you is that you have to be yourself. Maybe a lot of people have the misfortune to think they should copy him, but I was fortunate. I never had the opportunity to even think about imitating him because I was a nun. From the beginning I always knew it didn't have anything to do with imitating anybody.

There's nothing that you can hold on to. That's the job of the teacher to teach you that, so if they do, power to them. Then you

Bhikshuni Ane Pema Chödron leading walking meditation.

use the world as it is.

Question: Maybe it's a really good idea to find a teacher who's a creep, then you can sit there and observe how you can't stand him...

Pema Chödron: That wouldn't work. You have to surrender totally, knowing that the whole thing might be a fraud. If you don't surrender entirely, you don't learn anything. On the other hand, if you think that this person is going to save you, you don't learn anything. *(laughter)* So it's really, as they say in Vajrayana [Buddhism], that you're always in a state of panic. *(laughter)*

●

Question: I'd like to ask the teachers to speak to the issue of secrecy. There have been some teachers who have set up a model for how they should behave, and then when they don't [follow that model], they try to keep it under the rug. How do you think that should be handled?

Ruth Denison: Are you asking what should you keep under the rug? *(laughter)*

Question: I'm asking about the idea of secrecy within the community. You know, people don't do what they say. Teachers say one thing, then do another. Then they try to keep that a secret. It's not just about a teacher teaching students, but with your life, teaching your students.

Joanna Macy: The Lord Buddha himself gave an example of how you deal with that. Of all the world's teachers, he was the most anti-authoritarian. He had something to say about those religious teachers who developed a kind of "ritual technology" or special knowledge. He was known in his time as "the open hand." Nothing was kept secret. Of course you're raising another question about how much do we publicize what we know about people ...

Question: No, not just that. It's one thing to say that the Lord Buddha said that. That was the Lord Buddha many years ago and it may be wonderful what he said, but we're living in a bunch of communities nowadays where not everything goes according to the way the Lord Buddha said it should ...

Prabhasa Dharma: I'd like to address myself to that. When the Buddha started out, there were no rules. Then as people got together and the group got larger, things began to happen, then a meeting was called and a rule was made about it. That's how these 300 or 250 regulations came about [the monastic rules that Buddhist monks take as vows]. But Buddhism is a living tradition, and the tradition that I come from, Zen, is a living tradition—in other words, it adapts itself everywhere, in every country.

That's why I feel I can take the position of saying, well then, maybe we have to add to these rules, or take some away, or change them. That is the freedom we have and maybe the responsibility that some of you have mentioned you would like to take. Not just as, the teachers, but all of us—could sit down (maybe not tonight) and have a meeting about this and say that the situation calls for new regulations, or some additional regulations. I would see that as a constructive thing to do.

The Buddha did not start out saying there had to be 250 rules. He took situation by situation. For example, there was a monk who was the only son and he left home. In India people are married or promised early in marriage. His mother was worried that because he had become a monk, they would not have an heir to continue the family. She persuaded her son, she cried and begged him, "Please, let me bring your wife here, you can go into the bushes somewhere, but we need this child." So he broke the understanding that the monks had to live as celibates. Soon everyone knew what had happened. A meeting was called and a rule was made about that.

Buddhism as we live it is not a dead structure or a dogma. New situations arise and we have to find a way, a structure of how to deal with things.

Pema Chödron: In the very hierarchic sangha we have with my teacher, you learn what it means to be put into that position of hierarchy. Lots of people are put into it. It's part of your education in the sangha to play that role and find out what it feels like. Most people are extremely reluctant to take that seat, mostly because they've been criticizing "them" so long .... Also there is enormous loneliness, which teaches you about egolessness and not having anything to hold on to. It also teaches you about the flimsiness of "us" and "them." I can see a lot of the behavior that's causing such pain as coming out of not being educated enough about that role and how to play it.

"It is a simple fact that this work can only start with oneself."

Question: Is it necessary to be "us" and "them?"

Pema Chödron: Maybe it's not necessary, but since it exists in the world, not universally, it's interesting to learn about. If there's going to be enlightened society, you have to understand these things. Then what we pass on would be enlightened rather than neurotic.

Question: What I keep hearing from all of you is, we want to study Buddhism and walk the path and teachers may oppress us, but just be more assertive and work within the system. I keep wanting to see women teachers come out and get rid of the hierarchic focus and misuse of power.

Panel Discussion

Pema Chödron: The way things change is, you work with now. Revolutions usually are replaced by something of the same nature from the other side. So the way things change, for health's sake, is to work with right now.

●

Question: I lived in a community that did make decisions in a consensus fashion, and most of the people in that community became extremely close friends. But we put 90% of our energies into figuring out the most trivial things about how to live. Like, what time should the stereo be turned down and what time should we have household meetings, and how long did you let your yogurt sit in the refrigerator before someone else had the right to eat it. *(laughter)* Ultimately the community fell apart because, although we said we were there to discover peace and truth and create America as a peaceful place, we were talking more about yogurt. *(laughter)*

Question: I lived at Zen Center in San Francisco for six years. I feel there's a tremendous confusion about where a hierarchy is appropriate in a monastic life or in a teacher relationship. In visiting other centers, I found confusion on questions of daily life and the formal tradition in the zendo. It's very precious for people to dedicate their lives to keep it going, and for people to spend part of their lives to practice more intensely. But there's a lack of clarity and definition, and there's resistance to people leaving communities, of knowing when it's time for them to expand their practice and enter (the outside) community in a responsible clear way. Is hierarchy necessary in a monastic training situation?

Prabhasa Dharma: In Japan, I ended up in a monastery with only men, because the women's monastery had too few nuns and they couldn't do full-time practice. The structure was clear and it worked well. From the outside, if you were a foreigner and not experienced in Zen, you would think that being the Roshi was a powerful role and all the monks would shake (in fear) about it. But when I was interviewed, the Roshi gave me permission to practice with the monks. It was the first time they had let a woman in, but it was not his decision alone.

He called in the head monks, five of them, to drink tea with me. I was not told that it was a test, but it was. They watched me, how I drank tea, how I related to them, then they had to give their approval. The Roshi alone could not decide that. This was totally new to me. I thought he was the all-powerful Abbot, but he had to obey the monks as much as they had to obey him. All the monks must go through different positions of responsibility in governing the monastery. It's clearly laid out.

In America, it's a unique situation because we have mixed our communities, monks and laypeople practicing together. It is painful for those in training to be monks to have to do it "in public," so to speak. You have to go through a lot of steps, and you are pushed much harder because you are becoming a teacher. You should be able to do that in privacy, behind the walls of a monastery. I didn't have the luxury of that protection here. But we have a situation which is perhaps wonderful in this respect, that Zen and Vipassana and the other centers are open. Practice is available to everyone (not just monks and nuns).

This is our American situation. We'll have to call meetings where we sit down together, monks and laypeople, and decide how we're going to do this. It can't be solved by following teachers who don't have the experience of men and women together. ❏

Recommended Books

Jacqueline Mandell

Allione, Tsultrim. *Women of Wisdom.* London: Routledge & Kegan Paul, 1984.

Aronson, David et al. "Women as Rabbis." *Judaism,* Winter 1984.

Bolen, Jean Shinoda. *Goddesses In Everywoman.* New York: Harper & Row, 1984.

Bradley, Marion Zimmer. *The Mists of Avalon.* New York: Ballantine, 1982.

Brennan, Carla. "Sexual Power Abuse." *Kahawai.* Spring, 1984.

Brownmiller, Susan. *Against Our Will: Men, Women, & Rape.* New York: Bantam, 1976.

Buddhaghosa, Badantacariya. *Vissudhimagga,* vol. I & II. Berkeley: Shambhala, 1976.

Byles, Marie. *Journey Into Burmese Silence.* London: George Allen & Unwin Ltd., 1962.

Carmody, Denise Lardner. *Women and World Religions.* Nashville, Abingdon Press, 1979.

Christ, Carol. *Diving Deep and Surfacing.* Boston: Beacon Press, 1980.

Christ, Carol & Plaskow, Judith, eds. *Women Spirit Rising.* San Francisco: Harper & Row, 1979.

Claremont de Castillegi, Irene. *Knowing Woman.* New York: Harper & Row, 1973.

Curb, Rosemary & Manaham, Nancy, eds. *Lesbian Nuns: Breaking Silence.* Tallahassee: Naiad Press, 1985.

Daly, Mary. *Beyond God the Father.* Boston: Beacon Press, 1973.

Daly, Mary. *The Church and The Second Sex*. New York: Harper & Row, 1968.

Daly, Mary. *Gyn/Ecology*. Boston: Beacon Press, 1978.

Davids, C.Rhys. *Psalms of The Early Buddhists*. London: Luzak Co., 1964.

Demetrakopolous, Stephanie. *Listening To Our Bodies*. Boston: Beacon Press, 1983.

DeRohan, Ceanne. *Right Use of Will*. Albuquerque: One World Publication Co., 1984.

Dowling, Colette. *The Cinderella Complex: Women's Hidden Fear of Independence*. New York: Summit Books, 1981.

Eichenbaum, Luise & Orback, Susie. *What Do Women Want*. New York: Coward-McCann Inc., 1983.

Engler, John. "Theravada Buddhist Insight Meditation and An Object Relations Model of Therapeutic-Development Change." Dissertation, University of Chicago, 1983.

Falk, Nancy & Gross, Rita M., eds. "The Case of the Vanishing Nuns: The Fruits of Ambivalence in Ancient India." *Unspoken Worlds: Religious Lives in Non-Western Cultures*. San Francisco: Harper & Row, 1980, pp. 205-224.

French, Marilyn. *Beyond Power: On Women, Men, and Morals*. New York: Ballantine, 1985.

Frye, Marilyn. *Politics of Reality*. Trumansburg, N.Y.: The Crossing Press, 1983.

Garcia, Jo & Maitland, Sara, eds. *Walking On The Water: Women Talk About Spirituality*. London: Virago Press Ltd., 1983.

Gilligan, Carol. *In A Different Voice*. Cambridge, Mass.: Harvard University Press, 1982.

Goldenberg, Naomi. *Changing of the Gods*. Boston: Beacon Press, 1979.

Golson, Barry. *The Playboy Interviews With John Lennon & Yoko Ono*. Interviewer: David Sheff. New York: Playboy Press, 1981.

Gornick, Vivian & Moran, Barbara K. *Women in Sexist Society*. New York: The New American Library, 1972.

Gray, Elizabeth Dodson. *Patriarchy As A Conceptual Trap.* Wellesley, Mass.: Roundtable Press, 1982.

Gray, Elizabeth Dodson. *Why The Green Nigger: Re-mything Genesis.* Wellesley, Mass.: Roundtable Press, 1979.

Griffin, Susan. *Woman & Nature: The Roaring Inside Her.* New York: Harper & Row, 1980.

Gross, Rita M., ed. *Beyond Androcentrism.* Missoula, Montana: Scholars Press, 1977.

Gross, Rita M. "Women's Access to Dharma." *Vajradhatu Sun.* Boulder, Colo., Oct./Nov. 1982.

Hageman, Alice. *Sexist Religion and Women in The Church: No More Silence.* New York: Associated Press, 1974.

Hall, Nor. *The Moon and The Virgin.* New York: Harper & Row, 1980.

Hecker, Hellmuth. *Buddhist Women At The Time of The Buddha.* The Wheel Publication No. 292/293. Kandy, Sri Lanka: Buddhist Publication Society, 1982.

Henning, Margaret & Jardin, Anne. *The Managerial Woman.* New York: Simon & Schuster, 1976.

Heschel, Susannah, ed. *On Being a Jewish Feminist.* New York: Schocken Books, 1983.

Hopkins, Deborah. "Myth of Infallibility." *Kahawai* vol. XI. Honolulu, Winter, 1984.

Horner, I.B. *Women In Early Buddhist Literature.* The Wheel Publication No. 30. Kandy, Sri Lanka: Buddhist Publication Society, 1978.

Horner, I.B. *Women Under Primitive Buddhism.* Delhi, India: Motilal Banarsidass, 1975.

Horney, Karen. *Feminine Psychology.* New York: W.W. Norton & Co., 1967.

Inglehart, Hallie. *Woman Spirit.* San Francisco, Harper & Row, 1983.

Johnson, Sonia. *From Housewife to Heretic.* New York: Doubleday, 1981.

John, Da Free. *The Dreaded Gom-Boo.* Clearlake, Ca.: Dawn

Horse Press, 1983.

John, Da Free. *Nirvana Sara.* Clearlake, Ca.: Dawn Horse Press, 1982.

Kantner, Rosabeth Moss. *Men And Women of the Corporation.* New York: Basic Books Inc., 1977.

Kantipalo, Phra, ed. *A Treasury of the Buddha's Discourses From The Majjhima-Nikaya.* Bangkok, Thailand: Mahamakut Rajavidyala Press.

Kaplupahana, David J. & Indrani. *The Way of Siddhartha: A Life of the Buddha.* Boulder, Colorado: Shambhala, 1982.

King, Winston. *A Thousand Lives Away: Buddhism in Contemporary Burma.* Cambridge, Mass.: Harvard University Press, 1964.

King, Winston. *Theravada Meditation.* University Park & London: The Pennsylvania State Press, 1980.

Koller, Alice. *An Unknown Woman.* New York: Bantam Books, 1983.

Koltun, Elizabeth, ed. *The Jewish Woman: New Perspectives.* New York: Schocken, 1976.

Krishnamurti, J. *The Wholeness of Life.* San Francisco: Harper & Row, 1979.

Krishnamurti, J. *You Are The World.* New York: Harper & Row, 1972.

Lal, P. transl. *The Dhammapada.* New York: Farrar Straus & Giroux, 1967.

Lenz, Elinor & Myerhoff, Barbara. "The Third Coming; In Search of a New Spirituality," *The Feminization of America.* Los Angeles: J.P. Tarcher, 1985.

Leonard, Linda Schierse. *The Wounded Woman.* Boulder, Colo.: Shambhala, 1983.

Ling, Trevor. *The Buddha.* New York: Charles Scribner & Sons, 1973.

Lips, Hilary M. *Women, Men, and The Psychology of Power.* Englewood Cliffs, N.J.: Prentice Hall Inc., 1981.

Luytens, Mary. *Krishnamurti: The Years of Awakening.* New

York: Farrar Straus & Giroux, 1983.

Luytens, Mary. *Krishnamurti: The Years of Fulfillment*. New York: Farrar Straus & Giroux, 1983.

MacLaine, Shirley. *Don't Fall Off The Mountain*. New York: Bantam Books, 1970.

MacLaine, Shirley. *Out On A Limb*. New York: Bantam Books, 1983.

Marin, Peter. "Spiritual Obedience." *Harpers*. Feb. 1979.

Meiselman, Moshe. *Jewish Woman in Jewish Law*. New York: Yeshiva University Press, 1978.

Miller, Jean Baker. *Toward A New Psychology of Women*. Boston: Beacon Press, 1976.

Moon, Sheila. *Changing Woman and Her Sisters*. San Francisco: Guild for Psychological Studies, 1984.

Norbu, Thinley. *Magic Dance: The Display of The Self-Nature of the Five Wisdom Daikinis*. New York: Jewel Publishing House, 1985.

Norwood, Robin. *Women Who Love Too Much*. Los Angeles: J.P. Tarcher, 1985.

Nyanaponika, Maha & Story, Francis & Sister Vajira, transl. "Last Day of the Buddha," *The Maha-Parinibbana Sutta*. Wheel Publication no. 67-69. Kandy, Sri Lanka: Buddhist Publication Society, 1964.

Ochs, Carol. *Women and Spirituality*. Totowa, N.J.: Rowman & Allanheld, 1983.

Ochshorn, Judith. *The Female Experience and The Nature of The Divine*. Bloomington, Ind.: University Press, 1981.

Parrinder, Geoffrey. *Sex in the World Religions*. New York: Oxford University, 1980.

Paul, Diana. *Women In Buddhism*. Berkeley, Ca.: Asian Humanities Press, 1979.

Peck, M. Scott. *The Road Less Traveled*. New York: Touchstone Books, 1978.

Perera, Sylvia Brinton. *Descent To The Goddess*. Toronto: Inner City Books, 1981.

Phelps, Stanlee & Austin, Nancy. *The Assertive Woman.* San Luis Obispo, Ca.: Impact Books, 1975.

Pilgrim, Peace. *Her Life and Work In Her Own Words.* Santa Fe, N.M.: Ocean Tree Books, 1983.

Plaskow, Judith, ed. *Women and Religion,* revised ed. Missoula, Mont.: Scholars Press for the American Academy of Religion, 1974.

Prebish, Charles, ed. *Buddhism: A Modern Perspective.* University Park & London: The Pennsylvania State University Press, 1975.

Priesand, Rabbi Sally. *Judaism and The New Woman.* New York: Behrman House, 1975.

Racette, Catherine & Reynolds, Peg. *American Women: Our Spirituality In Our Own Words.* Santa Fe, N.M.: Bear & Co., 1984.

Reincourt, Amaury de. *Sex and Power in History.* New York: David McKay Co., 1974.

Rich, Adrienne. *Of Woman Born.* New York: W.W. Norton & Co., 1976.

Robertson, Roland & Holzner, Burkart ed. *Identity & Authority.* New York: St. Martins Press, 1979.

Rosenbaum, Max ed. *Compliant Behavior.* New York: Human Science Press, 1983.

Ruether, Rosemary Radford. *New Woman New Earth: Sexist Ideologies and Human Liberation.* New York: Seabury Press, 1975.

Ruether, Rosemary Radford. *Religion and Sexism.* New York: Seabury Press, 1974.

Ruether, Rosemary & McLaughlin, E. eds. *Women of Spirit: Female Leadership In Jewish and Christian Tradition.* New York: Simon & Schuster, 1979.

Rush, Anne Kent. *Moon/Moon.* New York: Random House, 1976.

Rush, Florence. *The Best Kept Secret: Sexual Abuse of Children.* New York: McGraw Hill, 1980.

Sayadaw, Mahasi. *Bara Sutta.* Rangoon, Burma: Buddhasasana

Nuggala Organization.

Sayadaw, Mahasi. *A Discourse on Vipassana.* Rangoon, Burma: Waida Sarpay.

Sayadaw, Mahasi. *The Great Discourse on The Wheel of Dhamma.* Rangoon, Burma: Buddhasasana Nuggala Organization, 1981.

Sayadaw, Mahasi. *Paticcasamuppada.* Rangoon, Burma: Buddhasasana Nygala Organization.

Schaef, Anne Wilson. *Women's Reality.* Minneapolis: Winston Press, 1981.

Schneider, Susan Weidman. *Jewish and Female: Choices and Changes In Our Lives Today.* New York: Simon & Schuster, 1984.

Shainess, Natalie. *Sweet Suffering: Woman As Victim.* New York: Simon & Schuster, 1984.

Soelle, Dorothee. *Beyond Mere Obedience.* Minneapolis: Augsburg Publishing House, 1970.

Soelle, Dorothee. *Suffering.* Philadelphia: Fortress, 1975.

Soma, Thera transl. "Kalama Sutta," *Selected Buddhist Texts* vol. I. Wheel Publication no. 8. Kandy, Sri Lanka: Buddhist Publication Society, 1963.

Spretnak, Charlene ed. *The Politics of Women's Spirituality.* Garden City, N.Y.: Anchor/Doubleday, 1982.

Starhawk. *Dreaming The Dark: Magic, Sex, and Politics.* Boston: Beacon Press, 1982.

Starhawk. *The Spiral Dance: A Re-birth of The Ancient Religion of The Great Goddess.* New York: Harper & Row. 1979.

Steinem, Gloria. *Outrageous Acts and Everyday Rebellion.* New York: Holt, Reinhart and Winston, 1983.

Stone, Merlin. *When God Was A Woman.* New York: Harcourt Brace Jovanovich, 1978.

Trevian. *The Summer of Katya.* New York: Ballantine, 1983.

Trible, Phyllis. *God and the Rhetoric of Sexuality.* Philadelphia: Fortress Press, 1978.

Wong, Mary Gilligan. *Nun: A Memoir.* New York: Harper & Row, 1983.

Woodman, Marion. *Addiction to Perfection.* Toronto: Inner City Books, 1982.

Woodman, Marion. *The Pregnant Virgin.* Toronto: Inner City Books, 1985. ❑

Contributors

Jan Chozen Bays, Sensei, is a pediatrician and mother of three, as well as a Zen teacher. She began sitting in 1973 with Maezumi Roshi at Zen Center of Los Angeles, where she raised her children and later taught, in addition to running the community's health clinic. She took lay Buddhist precepts in 1975 and in 1979 was ordained as a nun. In 1983 she officially became a teacher and was recognized as one of Maezumi Roshi's Dharma heirs. In 1984 she moved to Portland, Oregon to do a two-year personal retreat and sabbatical from teaching, while working and teaching part-time as a pediatrician. She is currently the teacher at Zen Community of Oregon, and is practicing pediatric medicine with a specialty in child abuse.

Bhikshuni Pema Chödron is director of Gampo Abbey, a traditional Tibetan Buddhist monastery for men and women on Cape Breton, Nova Scotia. She became a student of the late Vajracarya Trungpa Rinpoche in 1973. Formerly married, she has two grown children and was ordained as a novice nun by His Holiness Gyalwa Karmapa in 1974. She became a fully ordained nun in 1981, traveling to Hong Kong to take her final vows in a Buddhist temple. She was a teacher and co-director of Karma Dzong meditation center in Boulder, Colorado for four years. She has travelled widely throughout the United States and Canada on teaching tours, and in 1991 taught in England, Ireland, and Europe. She is the author of *The Wisdom of No Escape* (Shambhala, 1991). In the summer of 1992 she will be one of two principal teachers at the Vajradhatu Seminary held at Rocky Mountain Dharma Center, in Colorado.

A pioneer of Vipassana meditation, Ruth Denison has been teaching for the past twenty years in North America and Europe. She is founder and director of Dhamma Dena Desert Vipassana

Center in Joshua Tree, California, and the Centrum for Buddhism in Nichenich, Germany, where she leads both scheduled and self-courses throughout the year. Also a regular teacher at Insight Meditation Society in Barre, Massachusetts, she uses sensory awareness as a great support for the principles of practice. In the early 1960's she studied Vipassana meditation with the renowned meditation master Sayagji U Ba Khin at the Insight Meditation Center in Rangoon, Burma. In the following years she made several return visits to study with him, and is one of only four Western disciples to be given his permission to teach.

Dr. Joanna Macy, Ph.D., is an internationally known Buddhist scholar whose principal fields of scholarship are Buddhism, General Systems Theory, and social change theory. To help people find spiritual and psychological resources for effective social action, she has developed "Despair and Empowerment Work" and "Deep Ecology Work," and travels widely as a speaker, trainer, and workshop leader in the United States and abroad. She is author of *Despair and Personal Power in the Nuclear Age* (New Society Publications, 1983), *Dharma and Development* (Kumarian Press, 1983), and *Thinking Like a Mountain: Toward a Council of All Beings* (New Society Publishers, 1988), written with three co-authors. Her latest books are *World as Lover, World as Self* (Parallax Press, 1991) and *Mutual Causality in Buddhism and General Systems Theory* (SUNY Press, 1991). Currently she is Adjunct Professor at the California Institute of Integral Studies in San Francisco and Starr King School for the Ministry in Berkeley.

Jacqueline Mandell has been teaching Buddhist meditation retreats and classes internationally for seventeen years. She began her formal training in Bodh Gaya, India under the guidance of S.N. Goenka in January, 1972. Formally ordained as a nun, she was one of four Americans sanctioned to teach by the late Mahasi Sayadaw. She also practiced under the guidance of the Ven. Taungpulu Sayadaw at Taungpulu Monastery in Boulder Creek, California.

127

Her Rinzai Zen training took place at Mount Baldy Zen Center and affiliated centers under Joshu Sasaki, Roshi. She is currently practicing Tibetan Dzog Chen meditation. She taught at the Insight Meditation Society for six years and now teaches independently. She has lectured at the Harvard Divinity School and the World Health Organization. Her biography is included in: *Meetings with Remarkable Women: Buddhist Teachers in America*; *Turning the Wheel: American Women Creating the New Buddhism*; and *Buddhist America*. Married and a mother of twin daughters, she is also a writer.

Toni Packer was born in Germany and lived in Switzerland for many years, where she married an American student, moving to the United States in 1951. She studied psychology at the University of Buffalo and in 1967 became a student of Kapleau Roshi. In 1971 she was asked to begin counseling at Rochester Zen Center, and in 1976 took on additional teaching duties. Her encounter with the work of Krishnamurti crystallized a deep questioning of established forms and traditions. When she felt she could no longer work within the boundaries of the Buddhist tradition, she gave up being co-leader of the Zen Center in 1981 and founded a city center in Rochester. In 1985 she founded a country center in Springwater, New York, which was known as the Genesee Valley Zen Center for several years, and now is called the Springwater Center. Toni lives with her family in a nearby town, and together with a resident staff teaches at and administers the Center. She is author of two books published by the Center, *Seeing Without Knowing* (1983) and *What is Meditative Inquiry?* (1988); and one published by Shambhala Publications, *The Work of This Moment* (1988).

Barbara Rhodes, Ji Do Poep Sa Nim was one of Zen Master Seung Sahn's first American students and has been studying with him since 1972. She was given teaching authority in 1977. In 1988 she took precepts as a (lay) bodhisattva nun in the Kwan Um School of Zen. Rhodes Poep Sa Nim gives talks and leads retreats at centers of the School across North America. She is the guiding dharma teacher of the School, and the guiding teacher of Bultasa Zen Group in Chicago and Cypress Tree Zen Center in Tallahassee, Florida. A registered nurse since 1969, she works for Hospice Care of Rhode Island and for the Jewish Home for the Aged in Providence. Rhodes Poep Sa Nim writes on Zen for *Spirit of Change* and *Primary Point*. She helped found Providence Zen Center, and lived there for seventeen years, serving in a number of administrative capacities. While there, she initiated Providence Zen Center's ongoing series of Christian-Buddhist gatherings, and began a teaching dialogue with Native American teachers which she continues in Florida. She now lives in Providence.

Maurine Myo-On Stuart, Roshi, was raised on a farm in the Saskatchewan prairie in Canada, studied piano at the Sorbonne with Nadia Boulanger, and was a concert pianist for many years. After marrying and having three children, she encountered formal Zen practice in the early 1960's, studying with Yasutani Roshi, Soen Roshi and Elsie Mitchell. She was ordained a Rinzai priest in 1978 by Eido Roshi and in 1982 received confirmation as a Roshi by Soen Roshi during his last trip to the United States. She taught and led retreats at the Cambridge Buddhist Association from 1977 until her death in 1990. In addition to giving lectures about Zen, she started a zendo at Exeter Academy in New Hampshire at the request of the students. She left no dharma heirs. ❏

Practicing Centers
Affiliated With The Teachers

Jan Chozen Bays, Sensei

Zen Community of Oregon
c/o Jim Fuller
6323 SE 22nd Street
Portland OR 97201
(503) 235-8265

Bhikshuni Pema Chödron

Gampo Abbey
Pleasant Bay, Cape Breton
Nova Scotia B0E 2P0
(902) 224-2752

Ruth Denison

Desert Vipassana Meditation
    Center
Dhamma Dena
HC-1, Box 250
Joshua Tree CA 92250
(619) 362-4815

Jacqueline Mandell

Jacqueline Mandell
3220 East Galbraith Road
Cincinnati OH 45236

Toni Packer

Springwater Center
7179 Mill Street
Springwater NY 14560
(716) 669-2141

Gesshin Prabhasa Dharma,
   Roshi

International Zen Institute
   of America
P.O. Box 491218
Los Angeles CA 90049
(310) 472-5707

Barbara Rhodes,
   Ji Do Poep Sa Nim

Kwan Um School of Zen
528 Pound Road
Cumberland RI 02864
(401) 658-1476

Bultasa Zen Group
4358 West Montrose Avenue
Chicago IL 60641
(312) 327-1695

Cypress Tree Zen Center
P.O. Box 1856
Tallahassee FL 32302
(904) 656-0530

Primary Point Press is the publications division of the Kwan Um School of Zen. It has published *Ten Gates: The Kong-an Teaching of Zen Master Seung Sahn* (1987); the revised edition of *Thousand Peaks: Korean Zen — Traditions and Teachers*, by Mu Soeng Sunim (1991); and *Heart Sutra: Ancient Buddhist Wisdom in the Light of Quantum Reality*, by Mu Soeng Sunim (1991). It has reprinted *Only Don't Know: The Teaching Letters of Zen Master Seung Sahn* (1982).

The Kwan Um School of Zen is a network of centers under the spiritual direction of Zen Master Seung Sahn and senior teachers. The school publishes *Primary Point*, an international journal of Buddhism. More information about the Kwan Um School of Zen, including a list of centers world-wide, may be received by contacting the school at:

528 Pound Road, Cumberland, Rhode Island 02864
Telephone (401) 658-1476   FAX (401) 658-1188